WRITING FOR RADIO

For Pamela
who else?

WRITING FOR RADIO
Colin Haydn Evans

ALLISON & BUSBY

An Allison & Busby book
Published in 1991 by
W. H. Allen & Co. PLC
26 Grand Union Centre,
338 Ladbroke Grove,
London W10 5AH.

Phototypeset by Input Typesetting Ltd, London.

Printed in Great Britain by
Cox & Wyman Ltd., Reading, Berks.

ISBN 0 74900 007 4
The moral right of the author has been asserted

FOREWORD

Over the years I have produced a variety of different plays by Colin Haydn Evans: historical pieces on the Amritsar massacre and the Titus Oates plot; a Cockney Jewish comedy; a religious play set in an enclosed monastery; a drama that combined Morris dancing, fertility rites and a heartfelt criticism of the way multinational firms process seeds; and "Playing the Game", the play used as an illustration in this book. Yet this is far from being an exhaustive list, as he has worked with other radio producers on a yet greater range of plays. He is – to put it mildly – a versatile radio dramatist!

As a friend, and one of his producers, I was therefore both intrigued and apprehensive when invited to write this foreword. I owed it both to him and the reader to be scrupulously honest. I believe there are as many different approaches to writing radio drama as there are original – that is to say, good, radio writers. Would he – even with his versatility – be able to write something that would be genuinely helpful to aspiring, and even experienced radio dramatists? I need not have worried. As short as it is, I consider this the best book on the subject since Donald MacWhinnie's classic *The Art of Radio*.

In fact, I read the book with growing gratitude. All too often, producers like myself have to listen and reply to heartfelt complaints from writers about the delay in considering their scripts and how little constructive criticism one has given. Subjectively, of course, such complaints are quite justified, but by setting out so clearly the realities of a radio editor/producer's working life, Colin does a service to such producers – and even more so to aspiring writers.

I was delighted by his overall approach, concentrating as it does on what to omit rather than include. Not unlike Chesterton, who once remarked "If a thing is worth doing, it is worth doing badly", he advises the learners to listen to as many plays as possible – but particularly those considered "bad". It is only from evident faults that the writer can learn how to improve his own work. The accomplished play will seem seamless, with the hand of the artist initially invisible.

Colin is fond of paradox. He advises us to start with the simple and ordinary; that with which we might easily identify. A boy who plays truant, for example; or a successful and conventional dentist. Only then are we shown how to cast light on these everyday characters by supplying unexpected but truthful motives to their experience. In each case there begins a series of intriguing questions – the essence of good drama.

The book is eminently practical. Each chapter ends with an exercise in writing an original radio play. In one, for example, he advises us to let the characters – the heart and cornerstone of the play – grow only slowly. The play must not even begin until these characters have acquired a shape and life of their own. Their lives before, after and outside the action of the play must be clearly defined. As a producer, I find this knowledge can be enormously helpful in guiding and inspiring actors on the studio floor.

However, for me, his best advice is how to leave gaps in the dialogue, through which the listener – the image maker – can enter and do the essential work. He gives many delightful examples of how dialogue can be used to this end; both to avoid the obvious and to enrich.

I found this book a joy to read, and of great practical help.

Shaun MacLoughlin
SENIOR RADIO DRAMA PRODUCER, BBC.

INTRODUCTION

Writing for radio is different. Just how different I hope to show you in this book. The radio play is a form of writing where everything is done solely with the *sound* of words, nothing being seen save the effect they have on the mind and feelings of the listener. The audience is obliged to make up their own scenes, and, not surprisingly, they invariably turn out to be the most convincing. I make no apology for retelling the now apocryphal story of the little girl who was asked which she preferred – radio or television. "Oh, radio!" she replied, without a trace of doubt. "The pictures are nicer!" That's it in a nutshell.

This book will hopefully show the way towards creating just such effects in a planned drama script. It will take practice. You will have to learn to think with sounds, since what may look right on the page won't necessarily translate convincingly in performance.

Wherever possible I have used scripted examples to illustrate the various points. Given the basic talent, writing is much easier to do than explain, but with newcomers it's sometimes difficult to see that it's easier! Hopefully, this approach will overcome that problem.

The book is intended to be read as a practical manual. At the end of each chapter you will find a project to tackle. Ideally, you should work through one of these at a time, not moving on until you have managed to meet the requirements. It's not meant to look like writing by numbers exactly, but a structured approach is often the easiest way to come to terms with what is initially unfamiliar. Adopting this method should – by the end of the book – see you sitting on a completed play.

To keep theory close to practice, I will also be following my own advice at each stage of the way, devising and developing a script in tandem with your chosen idea. The result of these labours you will find in Chapter 6. In this way you will be able to see how the planned method evolves through a completed example.

Perseverance is the real key. A little done daily is far more useful than simply writing when the feeling moves. Inspiration has its place, of course, but it's a visitor that generally arrives uninvited in my experience. Leave the door open, by all means, but in the final analysis it's keeping regular hours that gets the job done. In fact, at the end of the day a good piece of work can often amount to little more than having had someone around to make the coffee!

Colin Haydn Evans
August, 1990.

1

THE RADIO WRITER

Each year the BBC produces literally hundreds of radio plays, often from writers whose work has never previously seen the light of day. In fact, in no field is new writing more encouraged – or wanted. Arguably, radio is the closest thing we have to a genuine national theatre. Uniquely, we still have intact a genuinely public service broadcasting system in this country, with all that implies. Writing for radio must go hand in hand with the defence of the medium, since each reflects the real worth of the other.

Like all markets, however, there are built-in editorial guidelines, and there is little point in submitting work that is not wanted. Few beginners consider this aspect – invariably to their cost. Good writing will always receive an acknowledgement, perhaps, but not necessarily a sale. So it's important to know the yardsticks against which to measure your ideas *before* putting pen to paper.

The current drama output of the BBC is divided broadly into four main "slots".

The Afternoon Play

This is perhaps the best outlet for the newcomer. Composed of plays of anything between 45 and 60 minutes in length, it represents the broadest cross-section of interest. Here you will find themes of all descriptions: the consequences of someone mislaying a supermarket trolley, the *angst* of a frustrated taxidermist, the marriage of two childhood sweethearts – on top of a bus. The subject matter is almost without restriction, even if the treatment is usually confined to well defined guidelines.

Thirty Minute Theatre

This is the slot at which most beginners instinctively aim, on the assumption that the shorter the script the easier it will be to write! In fact, the reverse is true. To structure a narrative that contains all the necessary dramatic ingredients in so short a space of time takes both skill and, for the most part, previous experience. The requirements, however, are much the same as for the Afternoon Play: a good storyline being the main order of the day.

Saturday Playhouse

The traditional "family" slot. Plays tend to be of the popular variety, 75–90 minutes in length, whodunnits and thrillers finding a natural home. This is no real place for the controversial, though more recently it does seem to be attempting a rather broader spread of wings. However, its basic function is to entertain; to do that convincingly and, more often than not, conventionally.

The Monday Play

This outlet (90 mins) is for the more serious theme: stories that provoke rather than mollify. If you have something strongly to say, this could well be the place to say it. But beware – ninety minutes is a lot of pages to fill, and to keep a story genuinely dramatic for such a period is not as easy as it might look in another writer's work!

Any script submitted to the BBC is read – though it's probably fair to say that some are more read than others. But providing you don't insist on writing in longhand on unnumbered pages using the backs of your current place of work's printed note paper, the system will virtually guarantee your efforts a fair

10

hearing. If professional readers were honest they would probably admit such a hearing may not extend much beyond the first dozen pages with some unsolicited scripts, but that's only because a working routine confined to four very close walls, hidden behind a pile of unread manuscripts, with occasional BBC tea as the only respite, is an inevitable prescription for a very pragmatic approach to things. Good scripts tend to grab you on the first page; bad scripts sometimes never even grab the author – and to a practised eye it shows.

There was a time when every script submitted received a written reply, commenting on how suitable (or otherwise) it might be in terms of a potential production. It's a genuine credit to the drama department that such a system survived for so long against such monumental odds. Shortage of staff – and so time – has curtailed this procedure somewhat, but anything of worth will still gain as much written encouragement as it merits, and in the case of a script showing real promise, an invitation to come in for a chat. I know of no similar opportunity for the new writer.

Anyway, you've finally found an envelope large enough to take your finished script, have carefully re-typed the page with the coffee stain, and are more or less prepared patiently to sit back and await results. But what is actually happening out there? You can safely assume someone will read what you've sent – but to what likely end?

The BBC drama department – like most other places of work – is composed largely of people, most of whom think, feel and behave as you do yourself (well, mostly). They are also generally overworked people. The result is that they do tend to take rather a long time to consider your script, if for no better reason than that they are doing the same thing on behalf of an increasingly large number of other people. So, if after six weeks or so you're beginning to wonder why you haven't heard a word it's because the process can sometimes take up to three months (I won't tell you the record). The answer, as all books on writing irritatingly advise, is to start work on something else in the meantime. And while you're adapting to that prospect, I'll comfort you with what is (prob-ably) happening to your first effort.

Assuming your script has passed through the initial filter mentioned above, it will reach the desk of an editor of the particular slot at which it is aimed – on the unlikely assump-tion that it has been aimed at all! Here it will be welcomed by yet another pile of yet-to-be-read scripts, all of which now at least qualify to be included on a rather long short-list. So you need have no fear that your play will ever grow lonely on its travels. At each step of the way there are always many of its kind to keep it company.

An editor's job is to buy a varied number of scripts each year to fill the slot for which he/she is currently responsible. Editors are a nomadic breed, tending to stay in the post for a year or two, and then moving on to fresh pastures. In this way the respective ground is kept sweet, as it were. Drawn from the ranks of the resident drama producers they are, of course, ideally qualified to judge the worth of the work received. On the whole, the process works very well, since the periodic change also subtly adjusts the bias of the bought input, each editor bringing to the job their own personal judgement. This makes for a genuinely creative mix in terms of overall output.

By the time an editor reads your script you are already a definite "possible". But here several other factors enter the picture – none of which may have much to do with the quality of your writing. Perhaps a play with a similar theme has recently been bought. (It's surprising just how often this happens – even with the most unlikely of plots.) Or perhaps the slot is temporarily over-bought. This thankfully doesn't happen too often, but it has been known. More likely, how-ever, is that your work shows genuine promise but simply won't translate convincingly into a valid production in its present form. Such a situation will almost certainly earn itself a written explanation of why this should be so – and, where necessary, an invitation to come in and discuss the matter.

This doesn't mean that they will necessarily buy the script.

It simply means that in their estimation you have potentially what it takes to deliver the goods at some future date. Whether you actually do so or not is entirely up to you. You are always on your own with writing, each and every day; a sobering fact to some, a genuine inspiration to others.

Success in this field, like so much else, is as much a matter of temperament as the ability to put words convincingly on paper. Where it differs from other pursuits, perhaps, is that the temperament required is invariably considered by other people as a trifle odd. But, as any psychiatrist will tell you (many of whom are writers themselves), it's much easier to prove a man mad than sane.

There is a chance, of course, that the editor may want to buy the script more or less as it stands. It does happen to quite a few plays in the course of a year, and after you have read – and practised – the contents of this book, there's no real reason why you shouldn't expect it to be one of your own.

A couple of different things can happen next. You can wait a long time for something to happen – or you can wait a very long time. It largely depends on a number of factors – none of which ever seem to justify an explanation. In fact, learning to wait is a very important aspect of selling written work. Over the years I have come to regard it as being second in importance only to the ability to actually punctuate.

Once given the go ahead, however, the play will be placed with an individual producer. He/she will then start in motion the process that will finally result in your writing reaching an actual performance. Depending on the producers current work-load this can (again) drag on a bit, but there comes a day when you receive a chummy little note from their personal assistant informing you of the dates of production, and you will venture forth in search of a studio you will almost certainly fail to find. The worst is now over – the totally unexpected yet to come.

New writers (and experienced ones even more so) sometimes tend to see the production of their work as uniquely their own, as if everyone else concerned were there merely to serve the always personal cause. In practice, nothing could be further from the truth. The recording of a play is very much a team effort, and to inhibit that process through egotism is to block the very means whereby words can effectively leave the page. Good writing is one thing – good playmaking quite another. The first can happen alone, the second needs the equal talent of others.

Good drama producers – something in which the BBC fortunately excels – are worth their weight in gold to a new writer. They take over your writing where you are obliged to leave off, moving it in a direction which may seem a little puzzling at first, but which nearly always leaves it improved. You may not know how they do it exactly – even though you are always invited to sit in on the operation – but you will almost certainly be grateful for the result. In my experience, over some years now, the final whole has always been greater than the initially written parts.

As I've said, authors are always welcome at the production of radio plays. They are genuinely felt to be an intrinsic part of the process – unlike in television, for instance, where they are often regarded merely as some necessary evil. Also, of course, they are very handy for producers to turn to from time to time and say (always with a smile): "I'm not sure that line quite works, are you?" At such times, you are recommended to put your money on the producer (at least for your first play!). You have reached the point in the process where his judgement is almost certainly better than your own – even about *your* writing. The initiative is now largely his. You are there to support his efforts on your own behalf. If you disagree with something, of course say so – but be certain you know *why* you object. It's not enough that the actor is sounding a bit nasal.

It is possible, of course, to find yourself with a producer with whom you simply cannot gel. This may be a matter of simple temperament, or, more seriously, where you wildly disagree with what he wants to do with the script. This has

14

never happened to me (in radio), but under such circumstances you would be well advised to stick to your guns. Radio has the advantage that the production process is usually geared to a simultaneous rehearse/record routine. This means that you can see what is coming before it actually finds itself irrevocably on tape – and so chip in accordingly.

Having said that, it must be firmly grasped at the outset that the sound you had in your head when writing the play will never be the one that finally appears in performance. In fact the likelihood is that the recorded version is going to be the better of the two, though this is not always the impression you may gain at the time! By the nature of the process, at the production stage you will never hear the play in its entirety; simply the individual scenes, often separated in time and place.

For this reason it's advisable that you make sure you know what your idea means in a broader context. This prevents you jumping to too many unjustified conclusions about how everyone else is handling it. If a producer wants to know what happens next where you feel you have drawn a final line, you should be able to give an answer. Sometimes actors like to know where a particular course of action is leading – even if you have chosen to leave it out. It helps them to characterise their performance as a whole. People will not be hearing your intended sounds, remember, they will mainly be hearing their own, and it should always be a mutual judgement as to the final result. A good producer weaves a play from the strands of such apparent differences.

Actors come in all shapes and sizes, of course – which is just as well, since plays do too. Except for buying them a drink at lunchtime and (hopefully) congratulating them on a wonderful job at the conclusion of the recording, the author has no direct access to the actors in terms of their actual performance. That's down to the producer. It is to him/her you address your remarks. In the main, actors recognise this rule, and usually steer clear of any discussion relating to the job in hand.

And that's really all there is to how plays get made; everyone doing what they do best in such a way that what was once simply one person's words on paper takes on the kind of character that the listener not only comes to recognise as that odd collection of circumstances we equally oddly insist on calling Life, but – ideally – may actually come to feel that what they have just heard actually enhances their appreciation of the matter. (Not that they usually bother to write in and say so, of course!)

In fact, it only leaves the one small matter of learning to write your own. But while we're involved with all that, start listening to other people's work. Not for entertainment, as perhaps in the past, but more to try and see just how the meat was put on the bone. Try to get your mind around what the author intended for the play, the motives for writing it in the first place – and how that was managed in practical terms. Was it obviously done, subtly so – what? Try to find out to your own satisfaction, armed only with this one rather heretical tip: don't listen to *good* plays – concentrate solely on the *bad*. The good ones will (at first) appear largely seamless, and not seeing the joins you won't know how it's done – a bit like a conjuror with a flat rabbit up his sleeve. The bad ones tend to reverse the process, making the shape of the sleeve unmistakably bunny-like, leaving you with plenty of scope for imagined improvement.

"Good" and "bad" mean different things to different people, of course, so for the purpose of this exercise (and that's all it is, so don't get madly frantic) assume that the good scripts are those which leave you green with envy and the bad ones wondering why they bothered to produce it at all. (But be sure it's not simply the subject matter you dislike!) This is not the most scientific of yardsticks with which to judge dramatic worth, perhaps, but then God forbid writing – of whatever kind – should ever become a science.

Summary

Although all radio plays are the individual statements of their respective authors, they nevertheless fall into distinct categories in terms of production schedules. In fact, it is possible to have a play rejected for no better reason that it simply won't fit any of the current slots. It is important therefore to become acquainted with the requirements of these various slots, and to structure your writing accordingly.

Exercise:

Listen to as many plays as you can, from each of the various categories, and try to identify the themes in terms of those outlets. See to what extent they overlap – and where the borderlines might exist. In this way you will begin to think like an editor. Keep a written record of your conclusions.

2

WHERE TO GET IDEAS

Most ideas beginners have for radio plays are wrong ideas. The common feeling seems to be that the more sensational the plot the greater the impact on the audience. More often than not the reverse turns out to be the case. Listeners tend to identify with what is familiar, and audience identification must always be your first consideration.

A safe axiom is that whatever starts out as *extraordinary* will have a very strong chance of ending up as very ordinary indeed. Good plots are always deceptively simple. In fact, newcomers to playwriting often experience a great deal of trouble when it comes to plotting – whether good or bad. "I have this urge to write", they say, "but I can't think of anything to write about!" The stumbling block revolves around the feeling that a potential plot should always be a full story from the outset. But it doesn't always work that way, stories often being the creative outcome of plots. There is no real reason why you should start writing with the entire treatment in mind. A simple theme is more than enough to set a suitable ball rolling.

Let's take a very basic example: boy meets girl, and wants to marry her. That's a time honoured idea, if ever there was one. Now let's turn it into a plot. Boy meets girl and wants to marry her – but can't. *That's* a plot. We've introduced a spanner into the otherwise neutral works; the very essence of good storytelling.

Now we need a development, since we obviously can't stay

with the situation as it is. There's always someone out there who will ask the awkward question – what happens next?

So, boy meets girl and wants to marry her – but can't because he's already married. Now we're well on the way. At this point the idea should be starting to ask questions of *you*; the obvious one being in this case – does the girl know he's married?

Almost without any extra effort on your part, the momentum of the idea now begins to take over, and the final structure should begin to emerge. You have a story on your hands.

Admittedly, this is rather a basic example, but don't be put off by that. Some of the greatest works of literature have as their basis some very simple themes. After all, with a few modifications, the above idea could well fit *Romeo and Juliet*! Drama uses only a very few basic themes – largely because that's all there is. The *treatments* are the true variables, and it is with these that writers mainly concern themselves.

In the above example, it's not too difficult to list several different reasons why the marriage cannot take place – and that almost off the cuff. Each one will potentially be a quite separate story, for a single theme can spawn any number of different treatments. This is the real art of effective plotting – always to make the unoriginal seem novel.

Still unconvinced? Well, let's develop the same idea along slightly different lines. Bob and Mary are planning to marry, but at the last moment Mary tearfully calls it off without any explanation. The situation as it stands remains fairly conventional; one that probably happens to someone every day of the week. There are no real ingredients yet to capture a listener's attention – at least not for the duration of a full play. To shift the balance we need to give our heroine a reason that fails to conform to the common expectations. Only then will we begin to engineer a valid story – if for no better reason than that our audience will have difficulty in anticipating the final outcome.

On that basis alone, it's obvious that if we reveal too much too soon we'll be back in the same position at which we started, and so will have lost the dramatic advantage. We always need to keep something up our sleeve – right to the end. The audience will only stay with us as long as there genuinely remains something to *find out*.

In terms of the actual writing, the character's hidden reason must always be at least as strong as the impact of the final resolution. In that way the audience will genuinely empathise with the reason when it finally appears, so – in this example – justifying the heroine's initial doubt. The outcome will be credible – and so convincing.

Let's say Mary has been previously married – unbeknown to Bob – and has suddenly discovered that her divorce (perhaps in some foreign country) is not legal. She wants to marry Bob, but can't – or tell him why. Not only have we now developed a workable conflict element, but she also has our sympathy. Her reasons for not telling Bob the facts should be kept back. The listener must never be told the whole story too soon.

Perhaps Mary has a visit from her ex-husband (without identifying him as such to your audience) and because of what goes on between them at the time, changes her mind about the forthcoming marriage. Not only is Bob puzzled, but so is your listener, and the only way they should be able to find the answer is to stay with it. Every square inch of your plot, and the way you choose to develop it, must be packed with ways of fostering that need in your audience. A good story is always a series of disguised questions (though they may sometimes look like answers), and only in the final scenes should it merge into a dramatic whole.

This approach to plotting has three basic strands: (a) the true conflict element should be hidden from the listener for as long as possible (but never artificially); (b) it should be as unlikely as overall credibility will permit; and (c) its dramatic effect should never be weaker than the final outcome of the plot itself.

The basic key is always to start very simply. Don't look for variations and sub-plots at this stage. These will develop of their own accord once the theme is firmly established, and will be twice as effective as a result. Just keep in mind that the theme starts the writing, and that the treatment is the writing itself.

So let's see how all this might work in practice. Make a short list of everything you did last weekend. Let's say you ran an errand for an elderly neighbour by strolling down to the local shops. No plot there, surely? Thousands probably do it everyday. The chosen theme is ordinary enough, perhaps, but the *treatment* does not have to follow suit. In fact, it is vital that it does not. *To the degree that the chosen treatment is untypical of the theme will be the strength of the conflict element in the story.*

So, to extend this idea into a potential plot, we must find something *untypical* to say about the situation – something that might confuse the expectations of the familiar version of events. Well, for a start, most people come back from the shops. So what if our chosen character doesn't reappear? There's our story – if only in embryo – and all we've done is made the central character an exception to an otherwise common rule. The subsequent treatment will be the way you, the writer, decide to answer the question that anyone with even a modicum of curiosity will now be asking – *why* didn't he/she come back?

Let's use another example to construct an analysis of a different idea's plot potential.

A middle aged character is digging in his back garden.
    (a)   Why?
        1. vegetable patch.
        2. garden pond.
        3. nuclear fall-out shelter.

    (b)   So?
        1. finds sealed tin box.
        2. unearths ancient Christian artifact.
        3. uncovers someone else's tunnel.

(c) Result?
   1. box contains collection of wife's old love letters from another man.
   2. disproves local archaeological theory.
   3. the tunnel seems to be heading towards his own cellar.

(d) Development?
   1. letters are from an old army pal from World War II.
   2. local vicar is the source of the theory.
   3. starts out down the tunnel.

(e) Resolution?
   1. realises the depth of feeling between wife and friend – and that the relationship was entirely innocent.
   2. vicar's reputation with locals at stake.
   3. realises wife's many hours of "wine making" in the cellar might have another explanation.

And we needn't stop there, of course. We can expand the basic idea even further.

(a) Why?
   1. digging a vegetable patch.
      (a) wants to go self-sufficient
         (a) wife disapproves (conflict?)
   2. garden pond
      (a) dreams of being the first to breed a particular kind of fish.
   3. uncovers someone else's tunnel.
      (a) finds two sets of footprints
         (a) recognises one set as those of his wife.
      (b) tin box from (b1) found in tunnel.

There's literally no limit to the detail you can add to each branch of the main tree, and with each strand you will be expanding a possible plot outline. At this stage it may be tackled purely mechanically, but you will reach a point where suddenly the whole idea comes together in a rush and you will know exactly where you are going. (Believe me, it *will* happen!)

In the above examples – and as I was writing – the idea of the man finding his wife's old love letters evolved quite instinctively for me into a story set during the last world war (told in retrospect) of a soldier paying a more literate friend to write his letters home to his wife. The letters begin as mere descriptions of the war situation, but as the friend's own needs are roused by the wife's replies, they develop into mutually felt declarations of love – which the wife, of course, believes are coming from her husband. After the war, the friend – coming to terms with the dilemma – honourably goes his own way, telling neither husband nor wife. For all these years the wife's feelings for her husband have been largely based on what was written all those years ago . . .

Fine – as far as it goes. But there still remain some unanswered questions. Why would she bury the letters? And how is the husband to realise what has genuinely taken place in terms of his wife's feelings? Back to the drawing board! Maybe she *did* know what took place, but like the husband's friend, felt it could never lead anywhere – something she would neither admit to him or fully to herself. And were her feelings down the years really for her husband? Perhaps she was simply living the dream that came to life only briefly, using it now as some touchstone to link her with the past. Alternatively, knowing the two men were very close, she might have been hoping that one day the other might be drawn back by the bond of friendship.

The technique is both simple and effective. There is only one basic rule to follow: start with a common situation that, in the writing, develops *untypically*. In this way you will automatically have both established and developed the all-important tension in the story, since the characters will be placed in a position that will dictate their behaviour in such

23

a way that they will unavoidably be in conflict with their surroundings and/or each other.

This method can also be employed to plot what goes on *inside* your characters, of course. Theoretically, a narrative could be charted solely with thoughts and feelings – but beware, such a scenario is not too popular with producers! Ideally, they like a mix of both, and, all things considered, they are probably right. A balance between motive and circumstance is a very sound combination in all storytelling.

So we now have a basic circumstance (theme) into which to fit our story (plot). The means whereby such a plot will develop will be the characters we choose to employ. Drama – good drama, that is – is always about people first and foremost, with events following on behind. All too often newcomers are inclined to use their characters as mere pegs on which to hang the plot. This is a common, but quite drastic mistake, since it effectively isolates those characters from the events in which they are made to appear, and the listener's chance of making the all-important identification with the thoughts and feelings that are the real pivot for the action is blocked. Audiences are not only interested in what characters do, but *why* they do it. Sound drama is much more about lifting surfaces than polishing them, and in the final analysis listeners are better captured by their own imagination than merely your own.

All of which brings us to the second part of the basic formula – what *is* a good character? In fact, the answer is very close at hand. You start with a person – *any* person. That's where we all start, after all. It's an unavoidable common denominator, the lens through which we focus the world in which we live. So let's take that recognition one step further with an imaginary example.

George has been a London bus-driver all his working life: industrious, never late for work – a model employee, in fact. As it turns out, he is a model family man as well: happily married for over thirty years and currently preparing for his only daughter's forthcoming wedding. Approaching retirement, he has nearly paid off his mortgage on his neat, self-decorated semi-detached. So far so ordinary. George may be a very nice chap and all that, but is an audience going to look at him twice? He may make an ideal neighbour, perhaps, but with the best will in the world he's not going to work too well as a main character in a piece of drama. Until, that is, we decide to introduce one *untypical* element into this otherwise ultra-conventional set-up.

At the top of his small house George keeps a room to himself – a locked room. No one other than himself has ever seen inside that room, and the curiosity his family once felt has long since evaporated with the passing years. It has now become their norm, the hours George silently – inexplicably – spends alone a mere unspoken acknowledgement between them all.

It is only when the daughter's future husband arrives on the scene that events start to take a slow turn. His curiosity is not unnaturally aroused by the rather odd domestic arrangements, and this in turn serves to re-kindle the family's old interest. Suddenly there is an urgent need to know what happens behind that locked door . . .

This technique is like placing a small drop of dye in a previously clear bowl of water. One single stir and the colour slowly starts to spread throughout the entire volume.

George is no longer simply a bus-driver to us now. His seemingly innocent life-style – through *implication* alone – has suddenly become suspect. For what reason exactly we do not yet know, but where once he may have made us feel comfortable, he now sows the seeds of unease. George has become a genuine *character* as far as an audience is concerned.

This simple approach (and by now you should be latching on to the fact that all the best techniques *are* simple) serves to illustrate just how an everyday person, chosen at random, can potentially carry the seeds for effective characterisation. As with plotting, we have started with the obvious and qualified it with the less so, the two sides of a common coin being made to clash in order to ignite a spark.

If appearances are to be trusted, George comprises everything we might expect of him. But good characterisation is never about the obvious. It always penetrates appearances, so making it necessary to introduce that small yet potent element of the unexpected. In this manner – and again very simply – what is perfectly ordinary can be given a very different hue. However conventionally George continues to behave, we are never again going to look at him in quite the same way. The worm has entered the once innocent apple, and all of a sudden we realise his behaviour is no longer indicative of who he is as a person.

All the main elements in a chosen story can be established through effective characterisation – that being, as we have seen, someone behaving (or thinking/feeling) contrary to the situation in which we find them. Only at the end of the story will it be necessary to bring the apparently contradictory elements together, so resolving the situation.

The real point of this exercise is that *any* character can be chosen and used in this way. It is simply a formula designed to exploit what we all individually expect of others in a given situation, what they expect of us in return – and the compromise both invariably must make in order that the situation remains mutually acceptable. Almost inevitably, the circumstances that arise will be genuinely dramatic – sometimes even comic. A bit like real life, in fact!

It is possible to plot directly from characterisation, without any prior knowledge of what is actually going to happen. A genuinely sound character *is* a story – automatically. You may wrestle with a potential plot for weeks, but if the people it portrays are not really credible (to you, that is) it will never convincingly lift off the page and into your listener's mind. After all, if the author is not fully convinced it's a bit much to expect someone else to fill the gap! Catch a listener's attention with a strong character, however, and they will go along with (almost) any given situation – if for no better reason than to find out how the character is going to react. In fact, well made stories could be said to be little more than a series of such reactions; someone creating a situation against which another responds. Good characters are *always* in conflict with themselves in the circumstances in which they appear. This may be through doubt, disappointment, circumstance, what have you – but their basic everyday stance in life is no longer holding sway, due to forces over which they have no apparent control at the time. It follows, then, that the listener must know of both these factors before the character will come alive. Who they *usually* are must be contrasted – naturalistically – with what they are now for the purposes of the plot.

It may seem odd to talk of fictional people as having lives beyond the requirements of the story in which you place them, but if they are to work in a credible fashion you, as their creator, should be in a position to know who they were both before and after the action of the play. The point at which they first appear in the script is not their logical birth, after all. In dramatic terms, it's simply the latest point in a long and almost certainly eventful life. What has gone before may not merit attention in the main action, perhaps, but it will almost certainly be a determining factor in how you represent the character. Try it as an exercise. Write a two-page description of a totally fictional character in some invented situation – and then repeat the exercise, using the same situation, but with someone you know well. Compare the two pieces. There should be a marked difference, and for no better reason than that one of the people concerned is *known*.

Fictional characters may be inventions, but they need not be any the less real for that. I have had some quite surprising exchanges with some of mine, and on occasion have simply sat back and taken dictation from the overheard conversation in my head. I didn't need to invent a single word. The characters had been so solidly built beforehand that their combined effect was strong enough to make the dialogue totally instinctive.

Now let's suppose I give you a character out of the blue and ask you to list some associated characteristics. We'll choose a middle-aged, successful dental surgeon, happily married with two daughters.

Your imaginary list might run something like this:

(a) plays squash twice a week.
(b) shares an interest in gardening with his wife.
(c) takes a foreign holiday twice a year.

Nothing particularly out of character there – until I also tell you that our new friend has, on three separate occasions in the past month, woken in the morning with the strong feeling that he is really someone else.

The feeling wore off as the day passed, but the conviction has grown increasingly strong with each fresh experience, until the day dawns when our character now knows, beyond any shadow of doubt, that the life he is leading really belongs to a totally different person . . .

And there I leave you! What are you going to do? Where is the actual plot?

Well, as it turns out, you needn't really do much at all. By introducing uncertainty into one character's life you have already done the same with every other character in the story. His family are obviously going to start thinking twice about it all, if for no better reason than the extreme change in his behaviour – and there is always the counter possibility that he may be right. You have only to follow each implication to an imaginative conclusion and you're home and dry. ("Only?" I hear someone scream!)

Yet by continually asking yourself questions in this way – and, of course, finding the answers – the plot is made to unfold *by itself*. Many successful stories have originated from little more than writers demanding of a given situation: "what if?"

. . . what if the new wife of an American President is a carefully planted, long standing KGB "mole"?

. . . what if a young Moslem girl has a vision of the Virgin Mary – in her local Mosque?

The technique requires no more than the talent to pose questions that are not commonly asked – preferably of everyday situations.

Of course, you could have chosen:

. . . what if a wife finds out that her husband is having an affair with his young secretary and, facing him with it, makes them both decide they must find some new meaning in their marriage?

. . . what if a husband finds out that his wife wants to find a new meaning in their marriage – and so decides to have an affair with his secretary?

. . . what if a husband and wife (who don't understand each other, but would like to) find out that their two children (who do understand them, but don't want to) have grown apart, and so decide to spend more time at home by giving up their weekend fell-walking?

Now I'm not suggesting such ideas couldn't be made to work – what has gone before has hopefully shown you otherwise – but only that, potentially, there are probably much better routes to take, even when planning to reach the same conclusions! The real point is that the eventual answer to our invented situations must always match the worth of the original question, just as its development into a final resolution must be genuinely credible. However extreme the chosen circumstances it must always seem to your audience that – given a slight shift in emphasis – it just might have happened that way. The greater the skill of the writer the greater the risk that can be taken in that direction.

By now you should have come to see that the conflict element – whether in plot or character – goes directly against the grain of the average response; a ready formula, in fact, for getting your listener to the end of your story. On the surface it may seem no more than a means of simply confusing any given issue – but that is really what all good stories are about! If your listener could easily anticipate the action of your play why would they need to listen at all?

Sound plotting is what the author makes happen to characters when circumstances temporarily defy the audience's expectations.

The key thing to remember about this planned discovery is that it cannot be made to happen for the listener unless it has first happened for you. In other words, if you are to make of the event a genuinely dramatic experience for your audience, don't expect to pull it off convincingly without breaking (or seeming to break) some new ground.

No writer can hope always to deal with what is genuinely new – still less what is actually original – but there's no real excuse for ever serving up something that isn't fresh.

Summary:

All good plots depend on conflict – and conflict is no more than the ordinary taken out of context. The best stories begin with mundane situations, develop through the unexpected, and resolve themselves by being credibly transformed by the journey in between. The "unexpected" is no more than the obvious with its surface lifted. It's the "sameness" of the world made temporarily unique by applying a fresh eye. No situation is immune to this kind of approach – the key realisation in effective story-making.

Plots are carefully contrived obstacles from which your characters extricate themselves by calling upon elements in their nature/circumstance that were hitherto unsuspected. Good plotting invariably *reveals* rather than *confirms*.

In similar fashion, vivid characterisation is simply the obvious taken out of context. A chartered accountant might well be considered a well educated man, for example – but what if he has been holding down a responsible position for years being merely numerate, with no ability to read or write? How? There's your plot!

Exercise 1:

Look through any tabloid newspaper and select three stories that would make good seed ideas for a piece of radio drama. (If you can't find them, look again – they are always there!) Choose one of the ideas and write a short account (3/4 pages) of the opening of a proposed play based on the idea. Don't use dialogue at this stage – just stick to the action. Now show this to as many people as you can persuade to sit still for ten minutes, and ask the question: "Do you actually *care* what happens next to these people?".

Keep doing this with as many ideas (or treatments of the one idea) until the bulk of your guinea pigs convincingly answer "Yes". (Beware members of family that agree solely on grounds of exhaustion.) At this point, you have the basis for a play.

Exercise 2:

Staying with the above idea, draw up sketches for the main characters of the piece. Now apply the same test to (advisably) a different set of guinea pigs, this time asking: "What do you really *think* of these people?" If they are stuck for words, or basically indifferent, repeat the process until they can almost immediately start chatting about the probable life-styles, appearance, ambitions etc of the chosen characters (other than those *you* have mentioned, of course!). In other words, you are looking for both a story and accompanying characters that have an immediate impact on the imagination of a number of different people. You're not out to alter human society at this stage – simply to stimulate genuine interest in a good story. That interest *must* be present before proceeding further.

3

EVERYTHING DONE WITH WORDS

The ability to write well for radio could almost be summed up as the ability to master the art of implication. By some strange quirk unique to the medium, the more you actually attempt to describe the less are your chances of communicating what you really mean. It becomes the dramatic equivalent of gilding the lily, of establishing the means whereby a fine balance is struck between deciding what your audience must discover for the play to actually work, whilst avoiding the more obvious ways of bringing this about.

Imagine writing a scene in total silence, for instance. Impossible? Well, maybe – but not so difficult as it may first seem. Silence – gaps between what people have to say to one another – plays a very important part in writing effective dialogue. It's precisely at these moments that the listener's own imagination is most stimulated. The words that have gone before, the words they are already anticipating will follow, merge to produce in their mind a picture that will either confirm or confuse their impressions. In either event, if you have done your job properly, they will be satisfied by the result, since the conclusion will seem *their own*.

So, starting with our completely silent scene, the first question to ask is: how much do I *have* to say – how many words *must* I use – to enable the characters to convey the required meaning? If you're ruthlessly honest with yourself, I think you may well find the answer to be – surprisingly few!

Let's take a practical example. A husband is telling his wife that he plans to leave her. The obvious opening would have him spelling out the fact of his going – setting the scene, as it were – with perhaps a following explanation of his reasons. We would then fall back on her reaction to the news, and the scene would draw to a natural close.

But what if we simply opened the scene with the wife's line: "Where do you plan to go?" At face value, this could mean any number of things. The husband may have announced he wants to spend a holiday alone – or perhaps he's off on a business trip and simply hasn't mentioned the hotel at which he plans to stay. The real key to the speech – the signal to the audience of the true character of the scene – will be the tone in which it is delivered. If this is angled correctly, it is the only pointer we need to tell the listener what has gone before. We have described nothing – but have implied all. It becomes a little like hearing things in the dark, and through some prior recognition being able to put names, shapes – actions even – to the impression gained.

In fact, this is a simple example of where a verbal signal (tone rather than speech) has been used to encourage the listener into an accurate assessment of the situation. We are relying on the audience's *own* imagination to set the scene – precisely what radio is all about. The listener is being indirectly asked to participate in the writing through the simple device of the author refusing to do all the work necessary.

In practical terms, there should always be places in the script where the writer should stick the small mental label "Enter Audience". If you never allow them this right the play simply won't work properly – if at all. No-one will necessarily be able to explain why exactly – both the writing and plot may seem capable enough – but as far as the listener is concerned something will be mssing: that "something" being their own presence in the treatment. The real art of writing is not simply serving the cause of your own imagination but that of those who choose to listen to what you have to say.

Now let's see how we can translate all this into some actual dialogue – using the above example of husband leaving wife. Firstly, by ignoring the given yardstick.

JACK: I'm sorry, but I have to leave.
JILL: But I don't understand – we've always been so happy.
JACK: I'm not sure I fully understand myself.
JILL: Don't you think you owe me some sort of explanation?
JACK: I don't know what to say.
JILL: It's someone else, isn't it?
JACK: I don't want to talk about that.

And now the recommended approach to the same scene.

JILL: (*shocked*) But – why?
JACK: (*quietly, avoiding her eye*) I'm . . . not sure.
JILL: (*very confused*) You must be!
(*HE MOVES TO THE DOOR, OPENING IT, BUT SHE REACHES IT BEFORE HIM, SLAMMING IT SHUT, NOW PLEADING*)
JILL: No! Tell me, Jack – please! I want to know. I don't understand.
JACK: I can't explain. These things happen – that's all.
JILL: (*desperately*) Jack, I love you! (*no response, then suddenly defeated*) Won't you even tell me her name?

Effectively, the same story has been told, but nowhere has the fact of Jack leaving been mentioned. In fact, only in the closing couple of lines is the ambiguity dropped. We may be fairly sure we know what it's all about – but can't be *certain*. The facts are presented through implication (silence) alone, relying on the tone with which the speeches are delivered to create the required effect. From Jill's shock in the opening line we know instantly something serious is afoot. This is no minor domestic crisis. And the stage direction before Jack's

34

response sets the scene for the tone of his reply. The voice sounds very different when there is full eye to eye contact – a fact the audience will unknowingly recognise as certainly as if they could actually see what was taking place. Jack's subsequent move towards the door, and Jill preventing him leaving the room with a change of tone that is now a plea, underlines what has gone before. It is only in the *final* line that our expectations are actually confirmed. In the previous version the *opening* lines does the job, so robbing the audience of any need to speculate.

You will see from the above example how much use was made of directions to preface some of the speeches. It may seem a little odd to talk about "avoiding her eye" on radio, but it does indicate – initially to the actor, and through them to the listener – precisely the effect you wish to create. The bald line "I'm not sure" could be made to convey any number of given impressions. What if the character had been angry, for instance?

It is possible to use the technique with equal effect in reverse, the point of the scene being stated from the off:

JACK: I'm leaving you for reasons you wouldn't understand – even if I told you.

JILL: (*bitterly*) You've always hated that rocking-horse, haven't you?

JACK: You simply don't listen, do you?

JILL: That's it, isn't it?

JACK: What?

JILL: Don't you understand – I'm fifty-eight years of age!

In this case, we know what is happening – but we don't know *why*. We have avoided a strictly black and white situation where it is obvious why the characters feel and speak as they do. Ideally, you should *always* be aiming to create a contrary impression, tensions arising out of situations that never quite seem to fully justify the unease. This puts your

35

audience in the unavoidable position of having to wonder about it all – preferably out of curiosity rather than annoyance!

It's always easy to see the reason why disagreements cause problems between people, of course – but what about *agreements*? Positive feelings can sometimes prove to be the cause of perhaps unacknowledged estrangement as much as their opposite, and this is an area where the writer would be more profitably engaged, if for no better reason than it is not commonly suspected. Always keep your eye open for the *dark corners* – every situation has them.

JOHN: I really do love you, you know.
MARY: I'd give anything to know what people mean when they say that.
JOHN: Do you love me?
MARY: You're wonderful!
JOHN: As much as I do you, I mean?
MARY: Perhaps we all mean something different. Could that be it, do you think?
JOHN: You always look as if you do.
MARY: Oh, I love it when I look like that!

Every line etched in mutual fondness – but can't you just sense the coming problems? (Well, you should!)

To acquire these techniques, as all prospective radio writers must, it's important to learn precisely how people communicate with one another. Not how you *think* they do, but by close observation of what actually takes place.

In practice, everyday conversation is composed far more of approximations than actual definitions: signposts more than destinations. For the most part, we tend to *imply* what we mean, the other person being invariably used as the medium of our *own* conversation.

Example:

JANE: He came out all in bumps.

SUE: I had that once.

JANE: Down one side of the face.

SUE: Not that I should be here by rights.

JANE: By Monday night I thought "it's the doctor for you m'lad"!

SUE: But they don't come out any more, do they?

JANE: That's my turn! It's been lovely talking to you, Sue.

None of the individual speeches are *directly* addressed to the other character. This element of self-interest – usually well disguised in normal social contact – should be kept carefully in mind when constructing realistic dialogue. Very often speech can contradict its own meaning; a fact that can be used to great dramatic (and comic) effect. It's the one area where you can always reply on the obvious as being highly unlikely! Even in extreme circumstances, people will rarely break with everyday mannerisms (except, perhaps, by simply screaming!). Yet beginners invariably assume that high drama always calls for similar dialogue.

So . . .

"My God, do you realise just how valuable a human life actually is? You don't, do you? You think shooting me will solve something – your problems, perhaps. I don't know. All I know is that life is precious – for you and me – and that by killing me you are never going to find any worth beyond it!"

. . . would be more credibly used as something like:

"Don't be daft – who'd want to go and shoot *me*?"

By *understating* extreme situations through the dialogue you enhance its dramatic impact – in the same way that overstating what is generally considered trivial can sometimes lead to a fresh insight into what was previously considered commonplace.

Let's use the above lines in a scripted example.

BILL: (*unbelievingly*) Don't be daft – who'd want to go and shoot *me*! (*no response, then with a growing unease*) You think I'm someone else, right? I resemble someone, perhaps? That's it, is it? (*no response, then the fear beginning to show*) I don't want to be shot over some mistake! I mean, that's . . . well, that's barmy, isn't it? I don't suppose even you . . . (*he tails off, the rising fear choking off the rest of the sentence. Pause, then very frightened, now pleading*) Oh – *please*!

When examined through written drama, these everyday verbal disguises can often transform what might previously have been seen as ordinary – even banal – into something genuinely riveting. In fact, invariably it is what is *not* said that carries the real weight of the scene, even though the inherent meaning must always be present, of course. These vital "gaps" create the opportunity for the listener's own imagination to enter, so allowing the means for that strange alchemy between writer and audience to take place.

Now if all this sounds rather technical it's because it's only theory. Practice is much easier to follow, as we shall soon see. The thing to remember for the moment is the importance of creating a genuinely *visual* approach to dialogue. It can't be left simply to the bald meaning of the words alone. After all, telephone sales-people are not trained to smile at the other end of the line for nothing! As an example of this approach, try the line "Why don't we just go to bed?" prefaced by the directions *WEARILY*, *SUGGESTIVELY*, and *ANGRILY* respectively. In effect, the character would be saying three different things. "I love you" may seem pretty unambivalent on the page, but what if you qualified it with *GIGGLING, HEARTFELT* – or *SNEEZING*!

By not taking words for granted, you open up all sorts of possibilities for their use, so making common meanings hint at less recognised directions.

Summary:

Bad radio tends to tell you everything. Each nuance and sigh is justified with a line of speech, almost as if the audience needed their hands held through each and every scene. They don't – and will grow very irritated (without necessarily knowing why) if you insist on doing it for any length of time. The real key is always to leave spaces in the narrative through which the listener can identify with both characters and action. These spaces, when used credibly, can become virtual doors in the otherwise impregnable walls of the writing, opening up a much wider view of the scene you wish to create. Ideally, the writing should be encouraging your audience to eavesdrop on their own imagination. Let *them* decide what to see – with only a minimum of help from you. In the final analysis, *imply* as much as you can get away with, and *describe* as little as can be tolerated.

Exercise:

Write short scenes for each of the following two situations, conveying the bracketed meaning for each *without revealing same in the dialogue*. Show the result to one of your now captive guinea pigs and ask them what they think the two characters are *really* saying to one another. Keep at it until you get the same approximate answer as the one given for each example.

1. A young man is telling his doting, widowed mother that he intends to emigrate to Australia. (*MEANING*: He can no longer live with her suffocating love and devotion.)

2. Jack and Jill are seen as not only the ideal married couple but the life and soul of every party – as in this scene. (*MEAN-ING*: They have nothing to say to one another when alone.)

4

AND SO TO WORK

By now, if nothing else, you will at least be in possession of a worthwhile situation. It may not look much at this stage, but it has been tried and tested on a small audience, and so potentially can be made to work. Now is the time to consider how we are to make it do just that.

Firstly, take a break – and give a thought to what you are actually setting out to do. "Write a play" you say? Well, yes – but why? You may well have a plot on your hands, but what do you intend doing with it? If you're not careful, it could very easily develop into a way of exercising all the known clichés on the subject. We want to avoid that, if for no better reason than that your audience will have already visited the place you intend taking them. Why should they reasonably be expected to go again, simply to give you the opportunity of putting words on paper?

Not that there's any problem in making the *plot* familiar: it's the *treatment* that must always seem different. The earlier this becomes apparent the better will it be for the play as a whole. In practice, this means that the first few pages must create the impression of the chosen theme whilst keeping in reserve the underlying incentive to pursue the action to the end. Ideally, an audience should never *know* why they are interested. You should catch them by intriguing them – not simply informing them.

Now look at your own idea. Stand outside, and ask yourself the question: "What do I *least* expect of this situation?" The answer won't come to mind very readily – by definition. You are looking for something that doesn't obviously exist, after all. Let's take an example:

SITUATION: A young boy consistently plays truant from school.

OBVIOUS REASONS: Bullying, bored, hates teacher, unhappy home life.

UNEXPECTED: Is an unsuspected child prodigy, daily visiting a local public library to gain knowledge the school cannot provide.

The real reason for the boy's behaviour is not dissimilar from the purpose of the main situation (to become educated); it is simply the least expected answer to his temporarily unexplained behaviour (conflict element). We could have given him any number of unlikely motives – but they wouldn't easily coincide with the basic premise of the plot. Going to school would have meant one thing – playing truant another. In this treatment they mean precisely the *same* thing – *and yet still manage to appear in temporary opposition to one another*.

Any given situation carries the potential for this kind of treatment, and must always be identified in an initial outline. Take a few moments (or longer) to find this element in your idea. It will be there, don't worry – it just won't be obvious. When you have found it, you will automatically have a story that works in purely dramatic terms. All the necessary ingredients will be present – unavoidably.

We now have a situation where *you*, the author, know where your proposed play is going – unlike your prospective audience. That's ideal. It means they are going to have to listen to all of it to find out – which is, of course, what you want. The point now arises: how and when do you tell them what it's all about? If you tell them in the opening scene, they'll know what the rest of the characters don't – and may decide the journey's not worth making. If you hold it back until the final scene you may run the risk of them becoming bored with the real reasons for your writing the piece in the

41

first place. So how do you know? Where's the yardstick that will tell you *when* to insert the necessary information – and how?

The answer lies in knowing how to structure the work so that each added ingredient displays its maximum potential. The method is to writing what blueprints might be to a motorway: it helps things go in relatively straight lines – hopefully in the direction of their final destination! True, you might have to watch your mental mirror for characters and events coming up fast in the outside lane (they don't always signal), but by and large it works.

So what *is* structure – in practical terms? It's not simply a plot, though a plot without it will seem a bit limp (unless your name happens to be Harold Pinter, that is). Its effect could be said to be the difference between keeping your best suit (your only suit, if you're a full-time writer) on a hanger or a hook. It keeps the *shape* of the original idea, moulding it to best effect in the final resolution, preventing the basic idea from rambling. Whereas a hook might well keep an article for a magazine in place, the hanger approach will happily cope with anything up to *War and Peace*. Even Harold Pinter uses them in this way, and, as everyone knows, he's got loads of suits.

A tree is structured. Barring hurricanes and overzealous pruning it has an inherent shape that is both produced and preserved through its own growth. That's how (good) writing should be. All too often would-be writers rush to paper at the first hint of an idea. In fact, this is the advice offered by most writing manuals: "get it down on paper before you forget." This is perfectly sound advice – up to a point. I've no objection to making notes, but I'm a very firm believer in the power of letting things simply gestate. In practice, this means leaving them quietly in the place they first arose. The moment an idea – or, more importantly, a character – is let loose on the world with actual pen and ink, a kind of "fixing" takes place. They can be changed after, perhaps – even altered out of recognition – but they will always be inherently the same as when they first appeared. The later changes will never be more than cosmetic.

Let's say I'm thinking of writing a play about an adopted, teenage girl deciding to track down her real parents. In a couple of minutes flat most of you could give me a plausible scenario on how to proceed (of course you could!) – but it wouldn't be your own. It would be derived solely from what you had previously heard about such a situation. I'm not saying it couldn't be made to work convincingly, but the structure would necessarily be contrived, since the main drive of the play would come pre-packed. But if you were to take time to actually think about this person – and the probable parents – perhaps asking all those more awkward "whys" that inevitably arise in any given human situation, both the theme and characters would need to deepen, if for no better reason than to take on board the enquiry. You may not be particularly looking for answers at this stage, but the simple fact of asking, of being genuinely curious about what might happen, gives life to what was previously only an unsuspected caricature. The characters are now no longer simply devices for telling a story, but living and breathing individuals who have rights and privileges equal to your own. You're actually relating, and through that encounter they begin to tell you who they really are and what they are about.

On this basis, you are dealing with something that has a very strong chance of turning out to be genuinely original – or as close as you are likely to get.

Now all this may sound a little fanciful – a mere mental exericse – but I can assure you it's a very concrete process, that definitely delivers the goods. It's only a matter of learning to take your imagination seriously. The standard, more obvious approach is to work from the outside in; a sort of "what you see is what you get." The more effective – more imaginative – angle lets what is going to happen arise out of originally not knowing at all.

So – what *are* you likely to find? The answer to that is that you will never really know. When you meet someone for the first time what can you know of them until they see fit to share your confidence? Fictional characters are no different. They won't confide in you unless you first make them real. The moment they begin talking to you – which is only another way of saying the moment you learn how to listen – the structure of the play is spontaneously established.

Are we then any closer to finding a planned ending for our story – *any* story? In fact, the real point is that we have effectively avoided the need to (consciously) look. Once the characters are real, you can safely leave it in their hands. There will be moments when you are tempted to interfere, of course, but that won't work for long. The people concerned will simply run out of words. That's the time to mentally apologise and return to the play *they* want!

Now if all this feels rather nebulous, I can only say that is the feeling that always accompanies the birth of any piece of writing. I make no apology for setting you at least one exercise that has to be done on the inside of your head. It's all a bit like photography; before you can "fix" an image permanently on paper, you have to choose where (and how) to point your camera, as fluid a process as the final result is still. What I am trying to show you here is how to avoid taking literary "snaps." Just as with the creative use of a camera, it does take a trained eye to go beyond the merely obvious.

The real structure of a play, then, is always derived from the characters. To emphasise plot above characterisation is to run the very real risk of having nothing – or very little – happen at all. Above all else, good drama is about *people*, remember; people in situations, certainly, but it's the real pulse of each character's personal nature to which the audience becomes attuned – whether they realise it or not. Only when that link is established, through empathy or otherwise, can the play begin to speak as it should.

For that reason alone, characters should never be chosen quickly. A name, perhaps – even a brief mental description – may well have to be the initial step (as in the earlier exercise) but the maturing must be left to its own time. Sometimes it happens all at once, but more often it's a quiet interior dialogue between early impressions and continuing thought. In fact, if a character turns out in the play in the same manner as first conceived it's a safe rule to assume they are not yet "alive." Good characters develop themselves – and will do so automatically if you give them the space.

In the given example – the girl looking for her real parents – we don't really need a plot. All we need to know – *really* know – are the people concerned. How long that will take is anyone's guess. It's up to "them." But if we are patient – are willing to listen more than dictate – they will eventually tell us "their" story, and in that telling we can begin to write a play worthy of whatever the situation turns out to be. If we try too early we are always going to come to someone else's conclusions. I'm not saying this isn't acceptable – even saleable – but it will never be the best of which you are capable. Why settle for anything less?

In the final analysis, then, you should never begin to write anything until it is actually finished! The writing should be the very final stage, no more than a recording of the facts that have already taken place in your head. Technically, things may be changed, of course – as furniture might be moved around a room – but the choice of house in which the furniture will live is decided. The original idea smiles at you – and perhaps for the first time, you are in a position to usefully smile back.

Given time, this approach becomes instinctive, but, like all things, at first some guidelines are often of help. So here's a quick way of systemising the approach; a tentative yardstick to hold against any piece of planned fiction to obtain the desired results. Effectively it's a "map" to get you through the largely invisible structure of the true story, whilst ensuring at the same time that the dramatic elements are always present. Don't worry if it looks a little dense on the page. If you could easily recognise the approach it would never work for you in the way it was intended! Think it through carefully, try it out on your own ideas, and you will soon see how simple it can be in practice.

For your main characters only, briefly compare the circumstances in which they find themselves at both the beginning and end of the story. These events should always *complement* each other. Based on that *alone*, devise a likely scenario for what might take place between. Then, in the writing, ensure that the actual events are at variance with your opening version.

In effect, this is a device for simply avoiding your first impressions about any given story. Unavoidably, you will always come up with a *novel* treatment. If you went looking for the suggested angle first, you would almost certainly find yourself sidetracked by the *expected* outcome.

If this technique is employed properly, drama will automatically introduce itself into the story, since you have placed your characters in temporary opposition to themselves and/or their circumstances, whilst still keeping the final resolution credible.

Summary:

Although there are perfectly workable ways a play can be developed in purely technical terms, it will always run the risk (often unsuspected by the author) of not gaining a true life of its own. In other words, it will be derivative. This is working "outside in". If the process is reversed, however – now "inside out" – we have a good chance of arriving at an unpredictable result: something approaching originality, in fact. This is the only real way of finding your own "level" – work that represents the best of which you are capable. Compromising at the beginning is often compromising everything that will follow – and who wants that?

Exercise

You should now have a basic idea on which to work – and, through the previous exercises on characterisation, the means to turn that idea into action. Write the first ten pages or so of the proposed script. If you feel unsure about how to go about it, revise the chapters to this point.

5

GOING WRONG – AS YOU WILL

Everyone goes wrong at the beginning; it's the only way of learning how to go right. The real problem lies in finding where it happens. It may be glaringly obvious in other people's work, but in your own it tends to be more elusive!

You may feel the play doesn't really work as a whole – but where and how? In this chapter we will try and identify some of the more common errors, and learn where to look for them. It will be extremely unlikely that your script doesn't suffer from at least one – if not all. So look carefully – and objectively – taking each stage in turn. Keep revising until you can read through without a single structural correction, however many attempts this may take. At that point it could be reasonably said you have done your best.

Overwriting

All beginners overwrite. Professionals do too, of course (otherwise script editors would be out of a job) but usually less often. It's virtually unavoidable, and something all writers are guilty of in their turn. It revolves around using too many words for too little effect, and is often difficult to spot, since writers often tend to see *all* their words as being very important indeed! As a result, a direct approach to correcting the problem is not always that successful. Everything looks as if it's carved in stone, with nothing willing to shift. I advise coming at it from a more oblique angle. That way the script doesn't see you coming, and surrenders its virginity with less complaint.

You may remember that in the chapter dealing with dialogue, we spoke of a potential scene beginning with total silence, and only then building the dialogue to do what we wanted. You were invited to ask yourself the question: just how many words does it take to make this character explain what he/she means? Well, there's nothing really stopping you applying the same approach to the play as a whole. In other words, just how many characters/scenes does it take to say what the *overall* theme intends? The answer is fairly predictable – and I don't need to see your script to know. It's about half the length of your first draft. Daunting, I know, but there it is.

Let's look at another example:

JOHN: Good morning, Peter. It's a fine day for a spot of fishing.

PETER: I'm glad you could make it, John. I hate sitting on the bank of a river all day on my own. By the way, did you remember the bait?

JOHN: After last time, I could hardly forget!

Reasonable enough, perhaps – at least on the page. But let's put the blue pencil to it and watch the change:

PETER: Thought you'd turn up – now the sun's out. At least you remembered the bait this time!

JOHN: You've never any good on your own, anyway.

We're getting closer, but we could go further still:

PETER: Why is it you only remember the bait when the weather's fine?

JOHN: You only ask me at all because you can't stand being on your own.

49

That's about as far as we can reasonably go. Why? Because further editing will push the whole thing into obscurity. We won't know what the characters are talking about – or why. That's your natural full-stop.

However, the editing has made something else happen; we have actually strengthened the characterisation. In the first version nothing of real consequence is happening at all – the exchange appears just about as bland as you can get. It tells us nothing about the people concerned. In the final draft, an edge has entered in. We get the distinct feeling that something is going on behind the words – something that the play to come may well reveal. Whereas excessive dialogue dilutes characterisation, when distilled – using soundly built characters – it can be made to mean *more* by saying *less*.

We don't need to know the characters' names either. They have no relevance to the exchange, and they sound rather stilted here. Also, as this is not the first time the two men have gone fishing together – which the conversation implies – John will know full well Peter's reluctance to be on his own. Peter is being made to say it solely for the *audience's* information – and it shows. Similarly, with the actual plan to go fishing, an opening reference to "bait", coupled with the suitability of the weather, surely suggests little else but a fishing trip, especially as we will be – unavoidably – following up with the fact. Always remember, we are out to *imply* as much as possible.

Now look at your own script in this light – page by page. Cut everything that is not strictly essential – "essential" being defined as that which is needed to save the page/scene from complete obscurity. Spare nothing – however treasured. At this stage we are simply counting the bricks; you can get round to repointing the building later.

At the conclusion of this exercise (which may take more than one go) you will probably be left with about half the length of the original script. If it's *substantially* more, repeat the exercise. Then re-read the script as a whole. Do you feel there is any improvement? If so, leave it at that and move on to the next stage. If not, then you have probably edited the wrong bits. We are not in the business of editing on principle, remember, but simply taking out that which prevents the story from being told to maximum effect. It's a bit like a prospective piece of sculpture. The figure (story) lies within the stone (writing) waiting to get out. But in order for this to happen a lot of raw material needs removing first.

Dialogue

As well as editing the script overall, it's likely that some attention will need to be paid to individual speeches, which will almost certainly be suffering from the same ailments. In all probability, and put simply, your characters will be talking too much!

Most of us communicate through a kind of verbal sema-phore – though it may not seem that way in practice. Try listening to a few conversations in a supermarket queue, and you will soon see what I mean. We make very broad assump-tions about other people's ability to read our own conver-sational signals, purely on the basis that common usage tells us it works. As a result, much of what we say to each other is characterised as much by "gaps" as content. But, in prac-tice, these do not consciously register, being "skipped" in favour of a more subliminal grasp of the overall picture. Unfortunately, when it comes to writing dialogue, this fact invariably goes unnoticed, and we often end up with charac-ters talking like Polytechnic lecturers over whether one prefers jam to marmalade!

Since you will be the instigator of your own problem in this respect, how will you know you are doing it? A trick that often works is to put yourself in the position of the character that is being *addressed*. Are you being told something

(a) you have been told before by the same character

(b) could easily have guessed anyway

(c) shouldn't know for the later purposes of the plot?

If so, there's a need to look at the other's speech and revise accordingly. Also, remember – as in everyday life – no two people talk to each other in precisely the same way. A conversation between a husband and wife over where they are going to spend this year's holiday will not sound remotely like the conversation the wife might have at work with her boss the next morning discussing precisely the same thing.

This is often one of the most glaring faults in beginners' scripts. Characters' speeches never vary in style, creating the impression (if the script didn't inform us otherwise) that they are always talking to a single generic person. The vocabulary, style and general tenor of their speech is applied equally.

Here's another little test you can apply to your script, then. With your *main* characters, is it always possible to know to whom they are speaking without the other character being named (or heard, of course!)? You won't be able to manage this on every occasion, perhaps, but it should be possible for the bulk of the exchanges.

Stereotyping

Characters should be made – not borrowed. Are yours? A golden rule when playing tennis is to never take your eye off the ball; with writing, it's the character. Whatever words you decide to put in their mouth, never for one moment take your attention off who is actually doing the talking. The moment you do, the dialogue will cease to work. You will have a stereotype on your hands, and the play will suffer accordingly. Of course, some characters invite stereotyping – the village vicar, the aged butler, the cowboy plumber, etc. The real point is that, however much your audience might expect a stereotype, the more inclined you should be to make it otherwise. Every character has a life beyond their mere appearance, and one that is generally invisible to the world at large. You have only to expose that hidden side – however fleetingly – to turn the convention around. The important thing to remember – as we have already established – is to effect the change from the inside out. In other words, let the outer stereotype stand, but let your audience know that *underneath* something else is taking place. It needn't be a great contrast – in fact, it should never be – but simply an unnoticed tipping of the scales in favour of the unexpected.

Check out *all* your characters (especially the small parts) for this factor. Are they real characters, as defined above, or are they merely pawns in the game of your plot? If the latter, change them accordingly, always making sure that such changes are *in* character. Giving a conventional village vicar a secret passion for speedway racing, for instance, though possible, is creating too great a distance between his outer persona and likely inner life (unless of course the play has something to do with speedway racing!). The overall effect is likely to be no more than amusing, since apparent opposites all too often tend to resemble one another. They provide no real way to get at the person beneath the skin. On the other hand, if our vicar is quietly nurturing a deep and long hidden crisis of faith – despite the orthodox assurances he continually offers his flock – you have a different matter on your hands. The contrast has been created within the established confines of the character, and so carries the necessary dramatic weight.

Signposting

The apocryphal story about signposting is illustrated by having one character in a script saying to another: "I want you to know that this gun I am holding in my hand is loaded"!

Now at face value, you can see the poor author's dilemma. He has this scene where one character is pointing a loaded gun at another – presumably with intent to do mischief – and not one member of his audience can see a thing! Obviously, the only way he can let them in on it all is by actually *telling* them. Well, maybe, but a lot can be lost in the translation, you see – as here.

The crux of the matter, then, is *how* do we convey the facts of a given situation without making it appear that is what we are doing? Of course you may feel that it doesn't really matter.

What's wrong with your listener knowing what you're up to? Isn't that what audience identification is all about? Well, no, not really. It's a little like a conjuror showing his audience how a trick works before the actual performance. It may still be amusing to watch, but the trick itself has completely lost its effectiveness. Written drama is full of such subterfuge – and you reveal it at your peril.

So what is the alternative? Once again, we fall back on our old friend – *implication*.

PETER: I suppose you think I'm bluffing. (*no response, then the faint sound of a pistol being cocked*) You always thought that of me.
PAUL: (*sceptically*) You want me to believe that it's actually loaded, is that it?

What have we gained here – and how? The same fact has been communicated, but in spreading it over more than one character, using a naturalistic response rather than a direct statement of fact, it appears more credible – and so convincing.

We could make up a small rule here: the less the number of characters used to convey the actual facts of the matter the less convincing will the facts appear. It's only when all other characters are totally ignorant of what needs to be said that there is any real justification in using just a single voice.

Go through your script and mark every scene that has been used to convey specific facts vital to the development of the plot. Now check to see whether any of the other characters in the same scene are aware of the same facts. If they are, have they been made to participate equally? In other words, has the required information emerged through an actual *encounter* or simply through a monologue?

Example:

JOHN: He may be right. She may come back of her own

accord. But they don't know everything do they –
the police. I mean, just because she left a letter
saying not to worry about her, doesn't stop you
doing it, does it?

MARY: They didn't seem too concerned, John.

JOHN: You've walked into that room of hers a thousand
times before. You must have thought it was a day
like any other. Everything in its place – life going
on as usual. How can you be prepared for a day
that makes your daughter leave home?

All the information here is handled by John. The other
character merely responds to what he says. Arguably she is
only present so that he can talk out loud – and so inform the
audience.

Now let's look at the advised approach:

JOHN: He may be right. I don't know.

MARY: It wasn't a – desperate letter. John, you can tell
when someone's desperate. The room – her clothes
. . . I mean, if she had . . .

JOHN: (*cutting in*) Are you saying you're not worried, then?

MARY: I'm saying I know our daughter. She wouldn't have
written that way if she didn't intend coming back.
That's all.

JOHN: You wake up, thinking it's a day like any other,
and then . . . this.

MARY: He didn't seem that concerned – the policeman.

In this instance, it's the *conversation* that puts us in the picture
– a very different matter dramatically.

One more rule then: none of your characters should seem
to *obviously* serve the purposes of the plot. They will, of
course – every last one of them – but it must never look that
way. Story and character must seem to arise mutually, each
complementing the other in such a way that the listener will

not pause to imagine it being better managed in any other way.

Structure

It's also fairly likely that your play will have begun – and finished – in the wrong place. You will have arrived too early for the opening and overstayed your welcome at the end.

Look carefully at the first six pages. The odds are that your real opening will be skulking around page four. You will have used the first three to "set the scene" – names of characters, backgrounds, what they do etc – and ignored the all-important point that a play must open by posing a question of its audience.

For instance, in a proposed piece about a married bank manager thinking of embezzling a large sum of money in order to run off with a secret girl-friend, we don't need to know that he works in a bank at the opening of the play. We don't need to know he's married, either. Or even that he has a girl-friend. It could simply open with the short scene:

MANAGER: I always wanted a house with a verandah. With red tiles – and a view out across an always blue sea. I've always wanted that, you know.
GIRL: Why have you always lived in Staines, then?
MANAGER: Why? Because that's where it is, my love. That's where it really is. Waiting. It always has been.
GIRL: Does your wife think that?
MANAGER: By this time next week, "Staines" will have given us that house. You, me – and a small corner of Mexico. What do you think of that, then?

In other words, never open with an explanation. We want a nice fat question mark facing us on the first page – the answer to which you will spend the rest of the play developing on behalf of a (hopefully) intrigued audience.

Check the opening pages of your script for the *real* opening. It may be on the first page – but I doubt it. Remember, you're looking for a question at this stage, not answers. They should come within the body of the script, and, going full circle, we return to a further query at the resolution of the action. This will be a different kind of question to that which opened the play. There we were demanding of our listener "guess what happens next?" The concluding query asks – now on behalf of well established characters – "can *they* guess what will happen next?"

At the end of the play the lives of the characters should imaginatively continue in the audience's mind, well beyond the planned action. It will be necessary to tie up the loose ends of the *plot*, of course, but what is not generally appreciated is that the characterisation will be largely open ended, and any attempt to plug the gaps here should be firmly resisted. That's strictly the listener's job.

Example:

JOHN: In a way I knew it would end like this. Just you and me, sitting here – talking as we are.

MARY: You had more faith than me. But you were right.

JOHN: I couldn't have been right without you.

MARY: What will happen now?

JOHN: We'll be happy. That's all.

MARY: You *were* right. Yes, we will be happy.

We are left in very little doubt as to what will happen here through the respective characters' sense of certainty. There's nothing wrong with that, of course, but a small hint of *uncertainty* widens the gap in the door through which the audience are made to squeeze – and so be present in the actual scene.

JOHN: I knew it would come right in the end. I always

	knew that.
MARY:	I hoped it would.
JOHN:	You must think so now.
MARY:	I *feel* it, anyway.
JOHN:	Isn't that the same thing?
MARY:	If happiness always made us *sure*, John, perhaps it would be something different altogether.

Ideally, a play should never end with a full-stop – but with a line of dots! In that way we are inviting the audience to continue the action in their mind, long after the final announcements have been read. A little like real life, in fact.

Summary

Overwriting occurs when you use too many words for too little effect. If your audience can *reasonably* guess at the prevailing situation, there is no legitimate reason to fill in the details through the dialogue. Only tell them what they can't possibly know – or guess. If you find this difficult to judge, try it on someone else. Until the penny drops, you should find that, in real terms, almost half of your dialogue is redundant.

Dialogue works all the better for being a little indefinite. Not to the point where no one can tell what your character is actually talking about, of course, but by always approaching the intended meaning of the speech slightly at an angle. Try to avoid straight lines in a script, both in plot and dialogue. They are rarely true to life.

Stereotyping makes your character lose credibility, since it reminds your audience of conclusions they have previously reached for themselves. The safest course is to take the stand that *no* character is typical – even when they look as if they are. Good characters needn't be complete exceptions to the rule, exactly, but they should always portray the rule in an unexpected light.

Signposting is to a plot what stereotyping is to characterisation. It states the facts in such a way that the action is robbed of dramatic worth. It comes about largely through underestimating your audience's capacity to understand what you intend saying. Never think they won't know what you're up to simply because *you're* doing the writing (they may even be ahead of you!). The real task is to *credibly* confuse that possibility by approaching the facts in a manner they would not have obviously chosen for themselves.

Structure, in an ideal sense, makes of each individual scene a full play in miniature. Of course it will rely heavily on what went before – as well as firmly laying the ground for what will follow – but it should also carry within itself something unique to the rest of the action. In practice, this is not always achieved, of course, but it is a useful yardstick for looking more closely at those scenes which do not really carry their weight. Opening scenes are particularly vulnerable in this respect. They often leave the impression of an author still undecided; not yet fully in his stride. The best approach is to limber up well before you start writing. Take a few mental laps round your intended plot, and when – and only when – you are firing on all cylinders, put pen to paper. How will you know? You will *need* to write, come what may.

Exercise

Consider your script to date in the light of the points raised in the currect chapter, and where necessary, revise along the lines suggested. Keeping in mind what you have learnt from the exercise, write the next twenty pages of the script.

6

THE SCRIPT

This chapter attempts to turn theory into practice – which is probably why it's the longest in the book! As promised, I have taken an idea of my own and developed it exactly along the lines advised. Your own script will seem very different (at least I hope it will!) but the principles employed should be the same. To help you follow the more important steps I have added a full scene by scene breakdown, outlining the mechanics of the matter. Reading this in conjunction with the actual script should answer any remaining queries.

The theme was the simplest I could imagine – and one often used. From that, I hope to show you how something quite different can be fashioned. It's a method that will work with any idea.

Title: PLAYING THE GAME.

Theme: A husband and wife don't understand each other because they don't understand themselves.

Plot: A retired office-worker has turned his wife into a "bowls-widow", spending the bulk of his time down the local club. She resents this, feeling he should spend more time at home – building a small wall along the bottom of their garden, for a start.

Resolution: They come to realise their way of staying apart was really an attempt to get closer – something that had remained largely unconscious for most of their lives together.

PLAYING THE GAME

A Play for Radio

by

Colin Haydn Evans

Colin Haydn Evans
(address and phone number)

Time: 30 mins

There may not seem to be too many things to be said about a title page, but an effective name for a play is something often overlooked. Yet, in some cases, it can actually be the spur for why your potential audience decides to listen at all. So don't rush into titling your script. Unless you have something very definite in mind, let the title emerge from the writing. Often something will spring to mind – perhaps from a line of dialogue. You will know when it happens. It will encapsulate the story exactly – and preferably a little obliquely. In this case PLAYING THE GAME sounds rather ordinary, but at the conclusion of the play we will come to see just how it lends additional meaning to what may initially may have seemed rather obvious.

The layout speaks for itself, though everything should be double-spaced.

CHARACTERS

BILLY ASHBY   (mid sixties)

DOT ASHBY   (mid sixties)

TRACEY   (early thirties)

ARCHIE MILTON (sixties)

THE PLAY IS SET IN A TOWN IN THE NORTH OF
ENGLAND.

THE MUSIC IS A BRASS BAND VERSION OF "THE
FLORAL DANCE".

All characters should be listed, however small the role. It is useful to indicate their ages, backgrounds, and, where necessary, the locale in which the action takes place. Obviously, if the play is set in the north – as here – it will be necessary to use actors that can convincingly affect the regional accent. Avoid large casts wherever possible. They are rarely justified.

If using music, specify precisely what you want – even to naming a suitable recording, if known.

Now we come to the script proper. Firstly, let's look at the layout. Each character's name is specified down the left hand side of the page, with the respective dialogue indented to the right. The individual speeches are numbered accordingly, starting afresh on each page. This is for purposes of clarification at the production stage. Instead of having to talk about "that bit on page 11 where thingamy is wondering about his wheelbarrow" it's must easier to simply refer to "Speech 4 on page 11". Of necessity, speech/scene numbers will be added at the production stage, whether you include them or not, but there's no reason you should begin your career unprofessionally.

Each and every scene either opens or closes with one of the following directions: FADE UP, FADE, CROSS FADE.

FADE UP. This direction always opens a scene, and must be qualified with either an "INTERIOR" or "EXTERIOR" – depending on the location in which the scene is set. This doesn't mean inside or outside the recording studio, but simply the kind of acoustic that will be adopted electronically to record the action. So you will be always opening with a FADE UP INTERIOR or FADE UP EXTERIOR, the former meaning indoors, the latters outdoors. This is further qualified by the actual location. So – in Scene 4 – FADE UP INTERIOR OF TRAVELLING CAR.

FADE on its own closes the scene. It draws a line across the ensuing action and prepares the audience for a switch to either another location, set of characters – or perhaps both.

CROSS FADE is combination of each direction. It acts as an acoustic bridge between two scenes, its purpose being to merge the action rather than make it distinct. In this instance, you will see I have used it to bridge Scenes 1 and 2. The final speech in the scene, however, must always be "prepared" by indicating what you intend. Thus, Speech 7 is preceded by the direction (FADING). This indicates that the closing stages of that particular speech will be faded down and merged with the opening (dialogue or effect) of the scene that follows. Without that direction you cannot have a CROSS FADE. (Although it could be used to precede a simple FADE). It's difficult to lay down set rules for when this direction should be adopted, since it's largely instinctive, designed to produce a specific dramatic effect. But as experience develops, you will find places in the action which demand this kind of transition. A play can get along perfectly well without it, however, and there's no problem at the beginning in ignoring it altogether.

Scene: 1	(FADE UP MUSIC, HOLD, THEN CROSS-FADE TO INTERIOR: ASHBYS' KITCHEN. BILLY AND DOT ARE JUST FINISHING BREAKFAST. A MOVEMENT OF CUP ON SAUCER ETC DURING THE SCENE)
1. BILLY:	(chewing) They don't go in for "walls" round here, Dot – they never 'ave.
2. DOT:	It's something I've always wanted – now you know that, Billy.
3. BILLY:	That garden fence has given us good service. That fence is nearly as old as me, is that fence.
4. DOT:	That's what I'm saying, isn't it?
5. BILLY:	How do you get sweet peas up a wall, then? Tell me that. They won't go. Sweet peas like a bit of something to cling to. It's their nature – clinging.
6. DOT:	It needn't be a big wall, Billy.
7. BILLY:	(FADING) It needn't be a wall at all, if you ask me.

In this particular script I have opened the action using a combination of directions. We FADE UP the music, HOLD (keep it running for a moment), then CROSS FADE (let the music slowly die whilst moving over to the INTERIOR of the Ashby's kitchen). For a moment, then, the respective acoustics of both music and kitchen will overlap, the first fading away behind the second as it comes to the fore. If the two characters – DOT and BILLY – had, say, been sitting

67

in their garden (as they are later in the play) the directions would have been CROSS FADE TO EXTERIOR, since the requirements of the acoustic would be different.

Directions – both in terms of the production requirements or to the actual actors' performance – are always underlined. The former will be in capital letters, whereas those addressed to the actor invariably precede the speech and are in lower caps. So Speech 1 – BILLY's opening line – is prefaced by (chewing). This simply indicates that a meal is in progress. We also need to know whether characters are standing, sitting, or lying down. Voices sound very different in each case, and just because your audience won't see your characters don't ever think they won't form very visual impressions over what they may (or may not) be doing at any given time. For this reason, at the actual recording, actors are often obliged to do almost as much as they say. The script therefore needs to reflect this requirement.

As we have seen in an earlier chapter, a (good) script should always open with a question. Not necessarily literally, as in a character's speech (though this can also be done, of course) but in the listener's mind. It needn't be very profound – in fact, it's far better if it isn't – but it needs to set the ball rolling convincingly. The audience must be made to feel "what next?" from the outset.

In this case, of course, we have little more than the matter of building a wall! Why does DOT want it built – and why is BILLY reluctant? Hardly an earth-shattering situation, perhaps – but then I did say to start small, didn't I? I'm only following my own advice!

| Scene: 2 | (CROSS FADE TO INTERIOR OF CROWDED BAR AT LOCAL BOWLS CLUB CLUBHOUSE. BACKGROUND CHATTER, SOUND OF GLASSES ETC. BILLY AND ARCHIE SEATED AT BAR, DRINKING) |

1. ARCHIE: Walls can be tricky, Billy, walls can. You never know where that sort of thing can stop. Look what happened in Berlin.

2. BILLY: All I'm saying is that I didn't retire after forty years to go piddling about with a load of cement at the bottom of me own garden.

3. ARCHIE: Quite right. (beat) Does that clock still go?

4. BILLY: Eh?

5. ARCHIE: Your retirement clock. (no response) The *firm*! Does it still . . .

6. BILLY: (cutting in, rather ruefully) It's solar-powered, isn't it? Won't work properly in a garage will a solar-powered. I'm not comfortable with a clock you can't wind, Archie.

7. ARCHIE: I'm with you there. (beat, then thoughtfully) Don't expect they have garages in Taiwan. It's British, isn't it – garages? (clink of glasses, FADING) Same again, then, is it?

Scene 3:   (CROSS FADE TO INTERIOR OF ASHBYS' KITCHEN. DOT AND TRACEY CLEARING THE DISHES FROM THE TABLE PRIOR TO WASHING UP)

8. DOT: Every day, by my reckoning.

9. TRACEY: He's always like it, Mum.

1. DOT: Can't see why. (beat) You feeling sick again, love?

2. TRACEY: I was just thinking.

3. DOT: Bowls is a man's game. That's what he tells me.

4. TRACEY: Ladies do it too. I've seen 'em.

5. DOT: Anyway, you make sure you keep that babby wrapped up. Never mind the calcium tablets and Jane Fonda exercises. Lambswool will get you through anything.

6. TRACEY: There's three months to go yet!

7. DOT What does Malcolm say, then?

8. TRACEY: About what?

9. DOT: The baby! What does he say?

10. TRACEY: (wondering) Well, he thinks it's . . . quite nice, really.

11. DOT: Some men don't know what to do, y'know. Your father didn't with you.

12. TRACEY: He was smashing, our Dad!

13. DOT: Not when you were a babby he wasn't. Didn't know what to do. "They don't behave like proper humans, do they?" Always saying that, he was. Sometimes he'd sleep in the garage.

1. TRACEY: You should join. The Bowls Club. Go with him.

2. DOT: Don't be daft!

3. TRACEY: Well, why not, then?

4. DOT: Tracey, love, can you honestly see your father and me down that place *together*? Well can you?

(FADE)

By the end of this scene much of the early gaps have been filled. We now know that BILLY is retired, is addicted to the game of bowls – and that DOT rather resents the situation. The scene is effectively set – ordinarily. The task now begins of how to make it otherwise.

Did you spot the new direction (beat)? This is the equivalent of a comma: a brief moment, not long enough for a pause, but nevertheless requiring an audible break in the rhythm of the speech. There are two other possibilities here. For a definite break (pause) – meaning precisely that – or where the character expects a reply and receives none: the equally self-explanatory (no response). These crop up later. Watch for them.

Note too how we have established TRACEY's marital set-up. This has been done purely by implication. Nothing directly has been said, but we get the drift, nonetheless.

Scene: 4 (FADE UP INTERIOR OF TRAVEL-LING CAR; BILLY AND DOT)

5. BILLY: (apprehensive) You could say it were just an outing, like. It seemed such a nice day, and so . . .

71

1. DOT: (cutting in) Billy, do ladies play bowls or
               don't they?

2. BILLY: (half heartedly) They try. A few. Now and
               again, like.

3. DOT: I think it's time we did something together,
               Billy.

4. BILLY: (worried now) How d'you mean?

5. DOT: (FADING) Even if it does mean playing
               silly beggars all over a bit of grass.

               (FADE)

This scene gives us one new direction – (cutting in) Not
surprisingly, this means one character's speech interrupting
another's.

Scene: 5   (FADE UP EXTERIOR; BOWLING
               GREEN. THE SOUND OF BOWLS
               BEING PLAYED. A MURMUR OF
               APPROVAL, AWAY, AT A GOOD
               SHOT;   SLIGHT   RIPPLE   OF
               APPLAUSE. DOT AND BILLY ARE ON
               THE GREEN, DOT READY FOR HER
               FIRST LESSON)

6. BILLY: (his voice lowered, anxious not to be over-
               heard) If Archie asks what you're doing,
               just say you're just down for the afternoon.

7. DOT: If you say that once more, Billy Ashby, I'm
               going to pull faces at everyone that passes.

8. BILLY: (a little alarmed) Now, Dot, don't go doing

72

anything I have to go and regret later. We're coming up to county championships. Decorum is what is needed for county championships.

1. DOT: Fat lot of "decorum" you're going to get with Archie Milton as President. He's had more Pot-Noodles down that Club woolly than rain down a roof. His mother always used to say he was a mucky eater.

2. BILLY: (hissing, desperately) Dot!

3. DOT: So what do I do with it, then? The – ball.

4. BILLY: (wearily) "Bowl."

5. DOT: I know that, don't I – but where?

6. BILLY: You roll it along the green, like. Aim it at that little white one.

7. DOT: Is that all? (no response) Like skittles, you mean?

8. BILLY: (with a groan) Roll it, will you Dot – everyone's gawping at us!

(PAUSE, AS DOT ROLLS THE BALL. PAUSE, THEN A FEINT CLICK AS BALL MEETS BALL, AWAY. BEAT, THEN BILLY'S REACTION; A MIXTURE OF SURPRISE AND DISGUST)

9. BILLY: (FADING) Yes . . . well, there you are then.

In the opening directions we have the term <u>AWAY</u>. This indicates sounds heard at a relative distance – in the background, as it were. <u>CLOSE</u> or perhaps <u>TO THE FORE</u> would indicate the opposite. (<u>A little away</u>) as a direction prefacing a character's speech, for instance, would require him to be standing slightly apart. Get into the habit of thinking in terms of space and distance when composing the action in your mind. It makes all the difference to the final result – especially when they are varied. (See the directions opening the next scene.)

Scene: 6   (CROSS FADE TO ADJOINING GAME, AWAY. MURMURING, SOUNDS OF BOWLS TO DENOTE PASSAGE OF TIME. THEN CLOSE; THE CONCLUSION OF DOT AND BILLY'S GAME)

1. DOT: (more interested now) So when you've knocked it with them all what do you do then?

(NO RESPONSE, THEN A SUDDEN DAWNING FOR DOT AS SHE REALISES WHAT SHE'S MANAGED; AN UNDISGUISED SENSE OF TRIUMPH)

I've *beaten* you, haven't I Billy?

(FADE)

Scene: 7   (FADE UP EXTERIOR OF ARCHIE'S ALLOTMENT. ARCHIE TURNING OVER THE EARTH, BILLY WATCHING)

1. ARCHIE: You've never had an allotment, have you Billy? (no response) A little patch of your own, like. (no response) It's a grand place for a shed, is an allotment. You can get yourself a primus in there and last out for hours at a stretch. A whole day, if you're inclined. A tin of beans helps, mind. You don't have to grow anything – unless you fancy. (beat) It's amazing just how many fellers round 'ere spend the bulk of their days in sheds of one kind or another. (no response) I don't understand it, anyway. I mean, what did you go and teach her for in the first place?

2. BILLY: (gloomily) Didn't teach her anything. She's got the knack, that's all.

3. ARCHIE: Every flippin' wood though, Billy. Not one out of place. She made you look like . . .

4. BILLY: (cutting in) She's got the knack! It's not my fault, is it? Not if she's got the knack.

(BEAT)

1. ARCHIE: Can't you un-knack her somehow? (no response) Something, anyway. I've already got my missus asking why some balls are bigger than others. It's getting serious, Billy. We can't have women all over the green. It's not environmental, for a start. And there's the championship coming up. I've already got me white flannels at the cleaners.

(BEAT)

1.	BILLY:	I've been a member of this club for how long, Archie?
2.	ARCHIE:	Man and boy, Billy – man and boy.
3.	BILLY:	There's no consideration shown.
4.	ARCHIE:	It's an art, is consideration. (beat) They think it's just a game, y'see. They don't see the underlying commyraderry. (no response) It were almost five years before Beryl would let me clean me white boots anywhere but the back step, y'know. (then, with a slight sense of victory) It's the kitchen now, lad. (a quick reservation) On a bit of newspaper, mind.

(BEAT)

5.	BILLY:	She's not particular with boots, is Dot – I have to give her that.
6.	ARCHIE:	Takes 'em different ways. With your Dorothy it's actual *playing*. (FADING) You might come to wish it *were* only boots.

(FADE)

Scene: 8	(FADE UP EXTERIOR: BILLY AND TRACEY SEATED ON A PARK BENCH)

| 7. | BILLY: | That's easy to say, but she's already beaten Arnold Roper in a friendly. I know he's not fully over his prostate, but he was really trying. You could tell – he'd got his blazer on. |

76

1. TRACEY: She's good then, is she?

2. BILLY: Well . . . she keeps winning, like.

3. TRACEY: Isn't that what you're supposed to do?

4. BILLY: Well . . . in a manner of speaking. But there're more to it, y'see. (then with a slight sigh) It's difficult to explain, really.

5. TRACEY: You mean you just want to keep it for the men.

6. BILLY: It's a sense of . . . well, of being together.

7. TRACEY: That's what she wants, Dad! She wants you and her to be together.

8. BILLY: I meant down the Club, love. Together, like. Listening to each other. It's – comforting, is that.

9. TRACEY: Mum listens.

10. BILLY: She does. I know she does. But it's a different sort of listening, y'see. Down the Club they don't mind much what they hear. To tell the truth, it's the only place where you can't make a prat of yourself. You've no idea how nice that can be at times, Tracey. The outside world's not designed for people making prats of 'emselves. Everything outside the Club is – well, it's bloody frightening at times.

(BEAT)

1. TRACEY: Have you told Mum that?

2. BILLY: No.

3. TRACEY: Why not?

4. BILLY: She'd not understand, love. Not proper.

5. TRACEY: Oh, go on!

6. BILLY: No.

7. TRACEY: She would!

8. BILLY: Now look – when did you last say something to Malcolm, then?

9. TRACEY: What? Don't be daft, Dad! Malcolm and . . .

10. BILLY: (cutting in) No – *said* something. Something that might make him put the paper down or switch off that flippin' computer of his. When?

(BEAT, AS TRACEY CONSIDERS THIS – ABORTIVELY)

11. TRACEY: (vaguely, evasively) I'm very fond of Malcolm, Dad.

12. BILLY: I know that, love. But you see . . . well folk can sometimes sometimes . . . well, rob one another, like. I've seen it happen. Done it myself, even. Not meaning to, of course. Nobody really means to. (beat) It's a cold place to be sometimes – on your own. So

we – wrap ourselves up in someone else to keep what little warmth we have. Natural enough. But sometimes *they* get cold for us doing it to them, y'see. We make them cold because we don't know how to keep ourselves warm.

1. TRACEY: I don't understand all that, Dad.

2. BILLY: (made a little self conscious by his frankness) Doesn't matter. (beat, then quietly, with feeling) You see, love, down the Club is – warm.

(FADE)

It's not really until this scene that we start to uncover what has, until this point, seemed a perfectly straightforward situation. BILLY indicates to TRACEY – and through her, to the listener – that there may well be other reasons why he spends so much time down the Club. In fact, is he really interested in bowls at all, we might reasonably begin to wonder?

Scene: 9 (FADE UP INTERIOR: CLUB HOUSE BAR; BILLY AND ARCHIE SEATED TOGETHER)

3. ARCHIE: It's there on the notice board, Billy. Large as life. She's used a felt-tip.

4. BILLY: There hasn't been a woman in the championship before, has there?

5. ARCHIE: They've always set up the tea, of course. No problems there.

1. BILLY: I'm sorry, Archie.

2. ARCHIE: Have you spoken to her, like? Explained.

3. BILLY: (gloomily) She wouldn't understand. Not proper.

4. ARCHIE: (with a weary sigh) There's your problem, y'see. Women and men understand different sorts of things, Billy. They always 'ave. Take me, for instance. I've never got the hang of biological washing powders. Try as I might it's a complete mystery to me as to what bits of clothes go with which packets. No shame in that. It's not something I hide. But a woman's not fond of being doubted. Puts 'em at a disadvantage, as they see it. So if you catch 'em out you get blamed something rotten. I've had more tongue-bashings from our Beryl for *her* being wrong about something than anything *I've* ever done. (beat, then sagely) Early fifties is the worst time, y'know. All sorts start up then. They get very chemical after fifty, do women.

5. BILLY: It don't stop 'em putting their name down for the championship though, does it?

6. ARCHIE: (a weary admittance, FADING) Aye, you're right there . . .

            (FADE)

Whatever we might have started to think about the revelations in Scene 8, this scene takes us right back into the action, and we are left with the all important "gap", into which – hopefully – the listener's imagination can enter the script. There's more to BILLY – and so the situation – than meets the eye . . .

Scene: 10   (FADE UP EXTERIOR; TRACEY AND DOT IN ASHBYS' GARDEN. DOT SORTING THROUGH A PILE OF BRICKS)

1. DOT: But it's only a *game*! I keep saying it, but nobody takes any notice.

2. TRACEY: It isn't, Mum.

3. DOT: What?

4. TRACEY: It's . . . something else. To them. It's not just a game.

5. DOT: Do you think these bricks would make a proper wall? Only a small one, mind. Eh? I know they've had cats over 'em and all, but they'd be all right up. What do you reckon, then? (no response) Look, love, men don't take anything serious that doesn't mean pushing a ball about someway or another. Doesn't matter the size, or which way it's going. Keep it on the go – that's the only thing they want to know. Sit them down in a room where they *can't* do it – and what happens? They switch on the flippin' telly to watch some other daft beggar do the same thing!

6. TRACEY: You didn't have to put your name down for the championship, though.

1. DOT: It were that Sugden woman! Her with the son at the Dental Estimates Board. After she saw me go and beat her Ted she was all over me to sign up. What could I do? (beat) Her mother helped lay out your Uncle Norman, y'know.

(BEAT)

2. TRACEY: He – talked to me today. (beat) Dad. (no response) He kept looking at his feet, Mum. You know how he does when he means something. Well, that's how he was. (beat) I think he means something.

3. DOT: What did he say?

4. TRACEY: He sounded a bit . . . well, lonely really.

5. DOT: (affronted) Well, that's not very nice!

6. TRACEY: I know.

7. DOT: What's he got to be lonely about, then?

8. TRACEY: It's something to do with the championship. (beat) I think it is.

9. DOT: He's got no cause, Tracey.

10. TRACEY: Sometimes folk make up their own cause.

(BEAT)

11. DOT: (a cautious prying) Is Malcolm lonely, then?

12. TRACEY: (wondering – for the first time) Shouldn't think so.

1. DOT: How would you know if he were?

2. TRACEY: (blankly) Well . . . (she breaks off) I wouldn't really.

3. DOT: I mean, there must be ways of telling, mustn't there? If nobody comes straight out with it, like. " 'Ere, I'm lonely" sort of thing. There must be – signs.

(BEAT, AS TRACEY TURNS THE MATTER OVER IN HER MIND, A LITTLE UNCOMFORTABLY)

4. TRACEY: He's got his Roy Orbison collection, like. He seems all right most of the time.

5. DOT: Well, what *is* being lonely, then?

6. TRACEY: He's going to catalogue it on the computer as a winter project.

7. DOT: Well?

(BEAT)

8. TRACEY: (unsure) Well . . . it's being on your own, isn't it?

9. DOT: Billy's not on his own. He's . . . (she tails off suddenly, as if the following words give her a sudden insight, then speaks the words slowly, meaningfully, half to herself) He's never been on his own. (beat, then suddenly anxious) 'Ere Trace, you don't think that's it, do you? (no response) He's lonely because he's never really been on his own?

(FADE)

Having been given time to wonder about it all, we are now back with the nitty gritty – one step further on through DOT's sudden insight (but still not a full explanation) at the closing of the scene. TRACEY's continuing picture of her "absent" marriage emerges as a kind of parallel to what is (perhaps) taking place with DOT and BILLY. But we still can't be absolutely sure. Hopefully, by now, the audience will want to know.

Scene: 11   (FADE UP EXTERIOR OF BOWLING GREEN. BILLY AND ARCHIE SEATED TOGETHER WATCHING A GAME IN PROGRESS. GENERAL SOUND OF PLAY, AWAY. HOLD A MOMENT TO ESTABLISH)

1. ARCHIE: (gravely) All bettings suspended, Billy. Only natural under the circumstances.

2. BILLY: (aghast) We've never had suspended betting before!

3. ARCHIE: (bitterly) Never had a bloody woman in the finals before, neither. (then suddenly remembering his place) Sorry, Billy – no offence intended. She's a smashing little woman is your Dorothy – under other circumstances, like. No one could say otherwise.

(BEAT)

4. BILLY: You just never know how life is going to treat you, do you Archie? Never know what's round the corner.

84

(BEAT)

1. ARCHIE: Tobruk. (no response) It was like that in North Africa. Flies, sand – bloody Montgomery in his flippin' caravan. We had it all to cope with out there, Billy. I tell you, if it hadn't been for the unfailing regularity of the corned beef I'd have lost all touch with reality on many an occasion. You have to keep a grip.

2. BILLY: (a rather forlorn hope) She offered to resign. From the championship, like.

3. ARCHIE: Her prowess has been publicly established, Billy. The committee have taken cognisance, like. Far too late now, lad. (beat) It's whether the precedent is to be carried forward – there's the real problem.

4. BILLY: (apprehensively) How d'you mean?

5. ARCHIE: (gravely) What's going to happen next year?

(BEAT)

6. BILLY: (horrified) She wouldn't . . . ?

7. ARCHIE: (cutting in, sagely) Success is a funny business, Billy. Once old Monty came out of his caravan, there was no stopping him. We were running up and down sand dunes night and day. Jerry were too, mind – but that's only because Rommel thought he was being successful too, y'see. (beat) I don't

expect they'd been a war at all if people hadn't wanted to go and be successful all over the place. Look how quiet a place Europe was before they all decided to go in for a spot of progress. The more they improve things the worse they get.

1. BILLY: Dot's not like that, though.

2. ARCHIE: (unconvinced) I dare say that's what Mussolini's family thought at the beginning. "He's a nice, quiet lad," they'd have said – and you can always rely on the trains now. Lots of folk start out that way, Billy.

(BEAT)

3. BILLY: What does your Beryl think, then?

4. ARCHIE: Never had much time for the Continentals. She hasn't travelled like me, Billy.

5. BILLY: About Dot in the finals!

6. ARCHIE: She says there's going to be a gap in the tea-rota! No grasp of the broader issues, y'see. I'm not unconfident, Billy. (FADING) It won't be the first time *I've* been in the finals, as you know.

(FADE)

In this scene we draw back again into the sub-plot. The real crux of the matter is being served in small doses – and irregularly. We sadden and amuse, alternatively. What is the real situation? Again, the audience are obliged to listen on in order to find out.

Scene: 12 (FADE UP INTERIOR; TRACEY'S LOUNGE. AWAY, MALCOLM IS WORKING AT HIS COMPUTER: AN ENDLESS SERIES OF BLEEPS THAT PUNCTUATE THE MONOLOGUE, GIVING THE IMPRESSION THAT TRACEY IS ACTUALLY CONVERSING WITH THE BLEEPS, WHICH SEEM TO RESPOND TO HER VOICE AND QUESTIONS IN LIEU OF MALCOLM)

1. TRACEY: (unsure, now that she has given it some thought) We . . . we do *talk*, don't we Malcolm?

(BLEEP)

You're not lonely, are you?

(A RATHER AGITATED SERIES OF BLEEPS)

Sorry, love, were you saving to floppy disc? (beat) I mean, if people were lonely it'd go and . . . well *show* wouldn't it? You'd be able to look at them and comment about something.

(BLEEP)

Have you got to "Pretty Woman" yet, Malcolm?

(BLEEP)

Don't you think it was a lot quicker when we just had all the records in a wire rack?

87

(beat, then rather pointedly) Anyway, I've decided to keep my recipe books as they are, if you don't mind. I can't see a disc-drive on top of the fridge, Malcolm. Not really.

(BLEEP)

I don't think computers have an exactly universal application, frankly. I don't. (beat, then a little sadly) I knew where I was with the salad garden once. You've gone and got my rotations in a right tizzy, you really have.

(BLEEP)

Oh, I'm not criticising! Everyone needs a hobby. I know that. (beat) Anyway, Mum thinks that you can be made lonely by being with the wrong person just as much as not being with anyone at all. (beat, then thoughtfully) If you can't live with yourself, it's a bit much to expect someone else to do it, isn't it?

(BLEEP)

Well, I suppose it is. (beat) She got right deep about it all – she really did. (beat) Malcolm? (no response, then with a weary sigh, rather vacantly) She wants to build this wall.

(A SERIES OF RATHER FRANTIC BLEEPS FROM THE COMPUTER, AS

IF SOMETHING'S WRONG. THE
ONLY SIGN OF EXASPERATION
FROM TRACEY NOW)

Malcolm, you've not gone into "Shift and
Exit" again!

(FADE)

Here everything is managed through heavy implication. Not
only is MALCOLM physically absent from the action, we
can feel he is also absent from TRACEY's life – something
TRACEY herself is struggling against admitting. The sounds
of the computer becomes a sterile go-between, so characteris-
ing the relationship – *without describing anything*. We are
encouraging the audience to draw their own conclusions here,
supplying just enough raw material to ensure they will leave
the scene feeling precisely as we wish. This becomes a continuing, parallel theme throughout the rest of the play (See
Scenes 14 and 16).

Scene: 13   (FADE UP INTERIOR; ASHBYS'
KITCHEN. DOT AND BILLY SEATED
OVER SUPPER)

1. BILLY: (<u>rather accusingly</u>) I never thought I'd see
it. I didn't. Archie Milton in tears. Beryl
said it hadn't happened since the Council
made him pull down his shed extension.
Eleven years that was. Shows what it meant
to him. Tears. All down his cream flannels.
He loves them trousers, does Archie.

2. DOT: I tried to lose, Billy – I really did! Tracey
will tell you how I really tried. But . . . well
I'm not sure I know how, y'see. You just
can't help hitting that little ball, can you?
It's so – simple.

89

1. BILLY: I've resigned. It's the only decent thing I can do.

2. DOT: (<u>rather shocked at this</u>) Oh, you must go on playing, Billy – you must!

3. BILLY: Resigned from the *committee*. Naturally I shall continue in my capacity as coach to the under-fifteens. (<u>beat</u>) Winning is not everything, Dorothy. You don't seem to have – well, grasped that side of things exactly. Y'see there's a certain style to the game that persists even in defeat. It takes years to perfect that. It doesn't come over-night, does style. You won't mind me saying so, love, but that was totally lacking in your own game, y'see.

4. DOT: All I could do was win, y'mean?

5. BILLY: To the unpractised eye, perhaps. But if you had watched closely, you would have seen the style used by many of your fellow competitors. It stood out a mile.

1. DOT: Pity they lost, though. I mean, with all that "style" you think they'd have won the odd game here and there. (<u>beat</u>) Archie Milton's "style" didn't seem much else but Beryl lending him her hanky for a good blow.

2. BILLY: Archie is a very emotional man, Dot. He was in North Africa, y'know.

2. DOT: Is that what he told you! Don't you take on – it were Bridlington – and a holiday camp at that! They've been going for years.

1. BILLY: He can personally remember Montgomery's caravan – and there's not too many that can say that these days.

(BEAT)

2. DOT: (puzzled) What are you on about, Billy? You can be a right fairy at times, you really can. (beat) Look, what do you want me to do – say I'm sorry for winning? Go down on me bended knees, is that it?

(FADE)

Scene: 14 (FADE UP INTERIOR OF TRACEY'S HOUSE. TRACEY CONTINUING HER MONOLOGUE WITH THE COMPUTER)

3. TRACEY: You remember, Malcolm.

(BLEEP)

You must! (beat, then a little subdued) I keep thinking about the wedding a lot lately. (beat) Remember them shoes the vicar wore! Mrs Shawcross said she'd seen them at the Church jumble the week before. (beat) He were a nice man, were the vicar.

(BLEEP)

Oh, he was! (beat) Pity he went and died. It's all guitars and laying on of hands now.

(BLEEP)

91

I'm glad we're having children, aren't you, Malcolm? (beat, then wondering, doubt-fully) It'll be much nicer than being on our own.

(BLEEP)

(FADE)

Only in the closing line of this scene is the surface of the play's real theme lifted again. Up to now we've been blowing hot and cold with our audience, as if trying to make them walk our path with a small stone in their shoe. Sometimes we allow them to stop for a while, so making it comfortable; then prod them to walk – with the feeling of the stone returning. There is a natural limit to this, of course – and that limit is reached when we have enough facts (but not explanations) in place to finally call up the final resolution.

Scene: 15 (FADE UP EXTERIOR: ARCHIE'S ALLOTMENT. DOT AND ARCHIE. IT IS RAINING HEAVILY)

1. DOT: Well we can't stand out here. We'll get soaked to our vests in this weather!

2. ARCHIE: There's nowhere else, Dot. We get used to it on allotment, y'see. It's . . .

3. DOT: (cutting in) What about your shed, then?

4. ARCHIE: (reacting to a major heresy) 'Ere now, hang on . . .

5. DOT: (firmly) Archie Milton – in that shed.

1. ARCHIE: (coming to heel) Right.

    (THEY MOVE TO THE SHED DOOR,
    IT OPENS AND WE MOVE INTO THE
    INTERIOR ACOUSTIC AS THEY
    ENTER, CLOSING THE DOOR
    BEHIND THEM)

2. ARCHIE: (pointedly) There's no sitting room for
    more than one.

3. DOT: I shan't be stopping.

4. ARCHIE: (nervously) Billy know you're here, then?

5. DOT: What's that got to do with anything?

6. ARCHIE: Just asking, like.

7. DOT: He doesn't, as it turns out.

8. ARCHIE: Right.

9. DOT: It wouldn't matter if he did, neither.

10. ARCHIE: (anxious to agree) 'Course not! (beat) Er
    . . . you won't mind me asking, Dot . . .
    er, Dorothy – you won't mind me asking
    whether all this is . . . well, *connubial*, will
    you? I mean, if Billy and you . . . well, I'm
    not the person to ask, really, y'see. I've
    always left that side of things to Beryl.
    Credit where it's due, like. She's the one to
    ask – if it's connubial.

11. DOT: Will you hear me out, Archie Milton?

1. ARCHIE: Oh, aye. You go right ahead, Dot.

   (BEAT)

2. DOT: You know Billy better than most. Outside the home.

3. ARCHIE: Always been mates, Billy and me – you know that, Dot.

   (BEAT)

4. DOT: (cautiously, a little self-consciously) Would you say he has a . . . well, a full life?

   (BEAT)

5. ARCHIE: (mystified) Full of what?

6. DOT: Archie, is Billy – *lonely*?

7. ARCHIE: Billy?

8. DOT: Are you deaf or daft?

9. ARCHIE: Billy *lonely*? Never!

10. DOT: How can you be sure?

11. ARCHIE: Well, *I'd* know, wouldn't I? I would. He'd say.

12. DOT: He mightn't.

13. ARCHIE: He would. He'd say, would Billy. It were Billy that helped put up this shed.

1. DOT: He's not said *anything* to you?

2. ARCHIE: Eh?

3. DOT: Has he?

4. ARCHIE: (very puzzled) I'm not with you on this, Dot. I'm not.

(BEAT)

5. DOT: (a sigh, then rather quietly, a little sadly, half to herself) So you do it to him too.

(FADE)

Scene: 16 (FADE UP INTERIOR OF TRACEY'S LOUNGE. TRACEY'S MONOLOGUE WITH THE COMPUTER CONTINUES)

6. TRACEY: (FADING UP) . . . and when he – or she! – grows up we'll all be able to talk to each other, won't we? Not all at once, of course – but one at a time while the other two are listening. Then it can be their turn. We can take it in turns, Malcolm. When there's three of us I expect there'll always be lots more to say. Well, it stands to reason, doesn't it?

(BLEEP, BLEEP)

(FADE)

Scene: 17 (FADE UP EXTERIOR OF ASHBYS' GARDEN. DOT AND BILLY SITTING TOGETHER RELAXED. A SOFT,

95

RATHER MELLOW MOOD BETWEEN
THEM)

1. DOT: I shan't do it next year, Billy. Not again. I shouldn't have come in first place.

2. BILLY: It'll blow over.

3. DOT: Will it?

4. BILLY: 'Course! Remember Tommy Wardle and that lass from the British Legion. Her that did the percussion. That blew over. (no response) He had a way with grass, did Tommy. The greens have never been the same since.

5. DOT: She's running a sub-post office somewhere down South. Married a man from the Isle of Wight.

6. BILLY: Seems a long way to go to be happy.

(BEAT)

7. DOT: (carefully) Are *you* happy, Billy?

8. BILLY: What are you saying to me now, woman?

9. DOT: You heard.

10. BILLY: (covering, with a self-conscious laugh) Bloody "happy"!

11. DOT: We've never asked, that's all.

12. BILLY: What?

1. DOT: Almost forty two years since you bundled me and that wedding-dress into the sidecar of that motor-bike for a weekend at Blackpool. Forty-two years – and we've never asked the other whether they were happy.

2. BILLY: (nostalgically) It were a cracker that motorbike.

3. DOT: You always go and pretend, Billy.

4. BILLY: "Pretend"!

5. DOT: When other folk see what you feel about something you always go and pretend it's not really there at all. You never want to be caught out . . . understanding.

           (BEAT)

6. BILLY: What's brought all this on, then?

7. DOT: Oh, I don't know. You and the championship, and . . . well, I don't flippin' know. That's why I'm asking, isn't it?

8. BILLY: I don't know what you're on about, Dot – I don't.

9. DOT: You're doing it now, y'see! You always want to go and seem . . . well, to seem less than you are, like. Even to me.

           (PAUSE, AS BILLY'S MOOD CHANGES, NOW MORE QUIET AND SERIOUS, UNCHARACTERISTICALLY OUT IN THE OPEN)

1. BILLY: It's what others want to think, isn't it?

2. DOT: (underline: encouragingly) What who thinks, Billy?

             (BEAT)

3. BILLY: Me Dad thought it. Everyone, really.
             You're brought up to think that way of
             yourself.

4. DOT: Who says that?

5. BILLY: Oh, aye! (pause) You know, first job I ever
             had they put me cleaning out old oil tanks.
             Winter it was – and twelve years old. My
             hands cracked in the weather, and I got the
             oil in. They came up so big I couldn't even
             wear gloves. (beat) Me Mam used to weep
             for the sight of those hands. But there was
             nothing to be done. My Dad had said it was
             going to make a man of me, y'see. (beat)
             But it didn't. It didn't at all. But I was the
             only one who knew.

             (THIS IS THE FIRST TIME DOT HAS
             HEARD THIS, AND BOTH THE SUR-
             PRISE AND SYMPATHY ARE
             REFLECTED IN HER VOICE)

6. DOT: But you always said you went straight into
             the works office.

7. BILLY: That were later. It were the oil tanks first.
             (beat) Offices weren't for "men", y'see.
             They did joined-up writing in offices, and
             made sense from pounds and pence. That
             weren't "men's" work. It were women that

kept the purse at home – and there was no good reason it should be different t'other side of work gates. (beat, then a quiet, but deep bitterness) I had to be made a "man" first, Dot.

(BEAT)

1. DOT: (quietly, an emerging tenderness) Have I not . . . have I not – looked at you properly, Billy? All these years. Have I not – seen you? Like your Dad. Is that what you're saying about *us*, then?

2. BILLY: (fondly) What are you on about now, lass?

3. DOT: Now don't you go dodging about again!

(PAUSE)

4. BILLY: Me Dad were the first, that's all. Don't expect *his* Dad saw him neither, if the truth be known. Mam didn't. He didn't her. Everyone just played the game, like. They didn't even know it were a game. (beat) I knew. I wanted to pretend too – but it wouldn't work. So I made up my own. My – own game.

(BEAT)

5. DOT: (cautiously) And young Dorothy Pickles – 42 Gordon Street. She was a bit of a "game" too, was she? (no response) Is that it, then?

(PAUSE)

1. BILLY: I was the only one who ever really saw me.
              When I worked hard at the oil drums so
              that they would think I was worth some-
              thing better, they gave me more drums to
              clean. In the office it were the same. When
              you did your best they made of it your
              worst. (beat) Then I found out. *Really*
              found out, like. People got on because they
              weren't themselves. They were always some-
              thing else: always what other folk expected
              of them, I suppose. (beat) It weren't until
              that moment that I knew I was going to be
              a failure in life. Whatever I did. No one
              wanted what I was – only what I couldn't
              pretend to be. (beat) I wasn't *ever* going to
              win, y'see Dot.

              (BEAT)

2. DOT: (a little distressed) Billy . . .

3. BILLY: (cutting in) I know what you're going to
              say. (beat, then very quietly) I don't know.
              That's the truth, I don't.

              (BEAT)

4. DOT: (sadly) Aye, you do. You know all right.
              (beat) I was just like the others, weren't I?
              You'd have been a "failure" to me too if
              you hadn't . . . played the game.

              (BEAT)

5. BILLY: I wish you hadn't made me say all that,
              Dot. I do.

1. DOT: (softly) Billy, lad – *I* failed *you*.

2. BILLY: (upset by this) No! Now that's not right! I won't have you saying things like that.

3. DOT: The Bowls Club was like a . . . shelter. (he starts to protest again, but she cuts over him) It was, Billy! That's where *you* play at nothing really going on. You can "fail" to your hearts content down there, can't you, lad? There's always next year's championships – and anyway, everyone knows it's . . . only a game. (beat) You can't really lose down the Club – ever.

4. BILLY: (upset) Dot . . .

5. DOT: (cutting in) No, hang on a minute. (beat, then slowly putting it together in her mind) So in I walk, don't I? Bold as brass. Thinking, I suppose, that because you were there and me here we were never together. But that weren't right, Billy – though I didn't know it then. (beat) You've missed something out, y'see lad. All these years. You've been – hiding. Like you do. Not talking as you really feel. What you've missed out was all that time I was . . . I was so . . . *fond* of you. Aye, you can look at your boots! That's what was happening, anyroad. (beat) I would have felt like that about you in your oil drums, when they gave you that daft clock after forty year, and every bowls final you lost – or maybe won. It doesn't matter, Billy. What you do, what you say – what you *don't* flippin' say. It doesn't matter. (beat) Perhaps I never did look at you as

101

you looked at yourself. Perhaps none of us can really do that – not proper, anyway. (beat, then tenderly) But I always looked at you the very best I had in me – and I never once wanted to look away. I don't know what you'd call that, but it's the only thing I have that I couldn't bear to lose. Not ever. (beat) Right, you can get your face off your boots now!

(PAUSE, THEN BILLY EXPRESSES HIS REAL FEELINGS FOR HER – HIS LOVE – NOT IN WHAT HE SAYS BUT IN THE TONE WITH WHICH HE SPEAKS – THE BEST HE CAN EVER DO)

1. BILLY: Wires would do, y'know. (no response) Along the wall, like. Sweet peas go up a bit of wire like nothing else.

(DOT HEARS WHAT HE IS REALLY SAYING – AND RESPONDS)

2. DOT: It needn't be a big wall, Billy.

3. BILLY: Well, it needn't be a small one, neither. It'll just be – a wall. We'll make it up as we go along.

4. DOT: (quietly, with great fondness) Wires would do smashing, lad.

(FADE UP MUSIC, HOLD, THEN FADE DOWN BEHIND CLOSING ANNOUNCEMENTS)

END

In the closing scene all the implications that had gone before are made to come home to roost. Previously we created a feeling that all was not how it seemed. Now we are saying that all that it means is more than it could ever seem. In other words, the *theme* is greater than the plot. BILLY and DOT were seemingly kept apart because they had no real means of telling the other that they really only wanted to be together. Through the action, and in the final resolution, we give them the means to do just that – uncommonly – so bringing the play to a satisfactory close. Remember the rather mundane disagreement over building a wall that opened the play? It now looks very different, seen in the current light. And the title itself – PLAYING THE GAME? It could simply have referred to the game of bowls, as the early part of the play tended to suggest. But as our characters open up we begin to see it means a great deal more.

The writing of this play has been faithful to all the rules and techniques we have explored in previous chapters. We started with something very commonplace, allowed the surface appearance to predominate for just as long as it took to establish the characters, then slowly prised open the situation to reveal something deeper underneath – the real theme behind the story. A measure of life emerged to take over the action – and it was a life we had not hitherto suspected.

This is the pattern I advise you to follow. It has a ready application for any and all situations. It doesn't depend on characters or plot – though, of course, it uses both. It's a *way* of writing rather than a means of determining what to write about. Using it as outlined will automatically create the necessary ingredients of a good story: interest, conflict, credibility.

Exercise

Compare your written script to date (around 30 pages) with the analysis of the printed script, above. Identify the parallels in terms of structure, characterisation and plotting. Revise accordingly. Write the remaining 20 pages (for a play of 45 minutes.) Repeat the process for the full script. When you feel you cannot revise any further, test the full script on as many guinea pigs as possible. If everyone reacts differently, ignore all comments. If two or more home in on similar points, re-examine these in the light of what you have learnt to date.

7

NUTS AND BOLTS

Agents

There'll come a time when, having stocked up on A4 paper, typewriter ribbons and a heavy-duty stapling machine, you'll feel that an agent should be added to the basic requirements. It happens to everyone – usually before they've even sold a word!

So, in response, here's the inevitable sobering thought – agents exist for your convenience only to the degree that you exist for theirs. No more, no less. If one side of the formula breaks down – or simply doesn't exist – there's little point in bothering each other further.

Books get published, of course, just as scripts get performed, but *which* script and at *what* time is often a totally unknown quantity as far as the newcomer is concerned. The agent is – or should be – in constant touch with both the changes in policy and those who affect such change; which means, at least in theory, their clients are too. Being informed in this way enables them to put forward suitable writers at appropriate times, long before the impending series (of whatever) ever sees the light of day. Invariably, by the time an unrepresented writer hears of potential work it no longer exists.

So an agent can be said to be a professional link between a writer and his market. Where a sale is successful they will take over the negotiation of fees, vetting of contracts, potential foreign sales and the like. For this they will (usually) ask ten per cent of the fee; a reasonable exchange, in my view. In fact, if you're not the best of negotiators when it comes to money, you might even make a profit on the arrangement!

There is, of course, an initial catch. An agent will usually only feel inclined to get you any work if you have already proved that you can sell it for yourself! Now this is not as unreasonable as it may first seem. Most firms are inundated with unsolicited material, the bulk of which is not only unsaleable, but, for the most part, quite unreadable. Just as a retailer would not stock goods on his shelf he felt could not be sold, so an agent would be foolish – and unfair – to undertake the representation of a new client if they were not first convinced that their work carried a future commercial potential.

The first move, then, is up to you. That initial, virgin manuscript has to be sold entirely off your own bat. This is often the highest hurdle you are likely to have to jump. At the beginning you are very much on your own, and the breakthrough can sometimes seem painfully slow in coming. In practice, professionalism is little more than sheer perseverance. Those who continue submitting work, sometimes against seemingly impossible odds, have a good chance of eventual success; whilst those who expect it all to arrive on a plate within a few months of sporadic effort are nearly always doomed to disappointment. After all, in what other profession could you reasonably expect such a quick return? Be willing to serve your apprenticeship – and only then expect some tangible recognition.

The agent a newcomer needs, then, is one who will take a genuine interest in the work submitted, will be honest in criticism, and is possessed of sufficient professional contacts to ensure that, if the work is of a suitable standard, it will reach the right person at the right time. There will be no written contract between you, and no charge will be made for handling unsold work. A reputable firm's sole source of income is derived purely from the commission charged on the sale of the clients' work. Any extreme exceptions to this rule should be treated with the suspicion they deserve. A few, smaller concerns survive solely on the fees charged for reading your work (often indifferently) and rarely, if ever, by actually selling it.

Long term, it's far better to be turned down by a good agent than accepted by a bad.

Income Tax

It's perfectly possible that there might come a time when the income derived from your written efforts attracts the eye of the Inland Revenue. This will almost certainly happen if you don't bother to inform them such an income actually exists (they like to be told these things, in my experience).

The range of expenses that you can offset against such income, however, are encouragingly broad, making the exercise often far less painful than you may have first imagined. It's one of the only situations I know where an actual spouse can be charged as a legitimate expense, for instance – assuming, of course, they actually assist you in your endeavours. The apocryphal: "This book is dedicated to my wife, without whose help it would have been written in half the time" lends a certain caution to the situation, perhaps – but no doubt even that lady qualified as a valid overhead in her day.

In fact, any outlay incurred in connection with the business of writing is fair game. Stationery, telephone, postage, reference books etc are the more obvious candidates, but there are a host of other, often ignored, expenses that qualify. Part of the expense of running your car can be offset against tax, as can travel and hotel fees. The purchase of a new vehicle can qualify as a capital allowance, a proportion of which can be used annually against your tax liability. The use of a room in your house solely for the purposes of writing entitles you to claim on its behalf in terms of cleaning, heating and lighting.

In the early stages, with perhaps just a single script sold, it may not be worth doing anything more than declaring the sale as extra income, but if you start selling work regularly it's well worth consulting a good accountant on the pros and cons of your position. The tax laws are constantly changing (how else would they catch you out?) and although both of the writers' reference books mentioned below have a very useful summary of the current position in their updated, annual editions, it's still wise to seek professional advice.

Whatever you decide, always keep detailed records, receipts and invoices. Each entry in your account book should be verified by an accompanying, official statement. This may be a bit difficult in cases of such things as postal charges, for instance, but such difficulties seem to be similarly recognised by the authorities, who generally seem quite happy to accept a (credible) assessment.

Value Added Tax

Virtually everything we buy – with one or two notable exceptions – has had its price inflated through the addition of VAT. If you voluntarily register for this tax (it only becomes obligatory beyond a financial ceiling few newcomers are likely to attain) you can reclaim the charge on any items/services purchased in connection with your labours. (It also means you are obliged to add the tax to anything you sell, of course.) At the end of each quarter you complete a statement sent to you by H.M. Customs and Excise, either forwarding – or reclaiming – the relevant tax for that period.

Is it worth registering, then? The answer to that largely depends on the level of your overheads. A full time writer would invariably be permanently returning more tax than he would generally reclaim due to the required level of his income, but on those few occasions when a substantial capital outlay needed to be made (new computer, car etc) he would be in a position to claim back the VAT involved – often quite a substantial amount. There is the chore of accurate record keeping, of course, but some might find that well worth the effort in terms of the potential advantage.

WRITERS' AND ARTISTS' YEAR BOOK (A. C. Black)

Published annually, this is often considered to be the freelance writers "Bible" – largely on the basis, I suspect, that until quite recently there was nothing similar available. Nevertheless, it's a genuine mine of information, is especially good on addresses for all and sundry, and well deserves a place on the shelf.

THE WRITER'S HANDBOOK (Macmillan)

A less comprehensive, but far more sophisticated version of the above tome, and my personal favourite of the two. Actually comments on the individual markets; the worth of which alone justifies the price of the book. Updated annually.

WRITING FOR THE BBC (BBC Publications)

Dry – but indispensable. A guide to literally everything they are prepared to buy, and – theoretically, at least – instructions on how to qualify as a potential supplier. Updated on an invariably occasional basis – usually whenever they get around to it.

Addresses

All drama scripts should be sent to: The Script Editor, BBC Radio Drama, BBC, Broadcasting House, London W1A 1AA. (And don't forget the SAE if you want it back!)

The rest is up to you – good luck!